ADVANCED GERMAN VOCABULARY

SECOND EDITION

HARRIETTE LANZER AND RACHEL PARIKH

The authors would like to thank Carolyn Parsons, Erwin Schaffer, Susanne Kucklei and Mike Short for their help with this book.

Extracts on pages 29 and 75 from Collins German Dictionary. Reproduced with the permission of HarperCollins Publishers.

First published in 1994 by:
Mary Glasgow Publications
An imprint of Nelson Thornes
Delta Place
27 Bath Road
Cheltenham
GL53 7TH
United Kingdom

This edition first published by Nelson Thornes 2001

02   03   04   05   /   10   9   8   7   6   5   4   3   2

A catalogue record for this publication is available from the British Library.

ISBN 0-7487-5781-3

Designed by Ennismore Design, London
Typeset by Tech Set Ltd, Gateshead, Tyne and Wear
Printed in Croatia by Zrinski

VORWORT

SIE HABEN SICH ENTSCHIEDEN, WEITERHIN DEUTSCH ZU LERNEN.

Dieses Buch wird Ihnen helfen, Ihren Wortschatz zu erweitern, Aufsätze zu schreiben und Ihre Prüfung vorzubereiten: Die fünfzehn Kapitel beschäftigen sich mit dem heutigen Leben in Deutschland und die Vokabeln und Redewendungen sind auf dem neuesten Stand des Sprachgebrauchs.

Unsere Vokabeltipps unterstützen Sie beim Vokabellernen. Sie entwickeln daraus eine eigene Strategie, wie Sie sich neue Wörter und Phrasen aneignen. Legen Sie dafür ein persönliches Vokabelheft an, in das Sie neue Vokabeln schreiben. Ein gutes Wörterbuch brauchen Sie natürlich auch.

Wir wünschen Ihnen viel Erfolg und viel Spaß!

Abkürzungen:

m	*masculine*
f	*feminine*
n	*neuter*
pl	*plural*
inf	*informal*

Pluralformen sind in Klammern angegeben:

der Kindergarten (⸚) = die Kindergärten

die Schule (n) = die Schulen

das Thema (-men) = die Themen

INHALT

ARBEITSWELT

STELLENSUCHE

die Absage (n)	rejection
das Anschreiben (-)	covering letter
der/die Arbeitssuchende (n)	job hunter
der Arbeitsvertrag (⸚ e)	work contract
der/die Berufsanfänger/in (-/nen)	
	career starter
die Berufsaussichten (pl)	job prospects
die Berufserfahrung	
	professional experience
der/die Bewerber/in (-/nen)	applicant
die Bewerbung (en)	application
das Bewerbungsformular (e)	
	application form
die Bewerbungsunterlagen (pl)	
	application papers
der Lebenslauf (⸚ e)	curriculum vitae

der Manteltarifvertrag (⸚ e)	
	conditions of employment
die Personalabteilung (en)	
	human resources department
das Stellenangebot (e)	job offer
die Stellenanzeige (n)	job advert
die Stellenbeschreibung	
	job description
der Stellenmarkt	job market
das Stellenprofil (e)	job profile
das Vorstellungsgespräch (e)	interview
das Zeugnis (se)	testimonial

IM BÜRO

der Anruf (e)	phone call
der Anrufbeantworter (-)	answerphone
das Callcenter	call centre

sich (online) um eine Stelle bei X bewerben	to apply for a job at X (online)
X dient mir als Referenz	X is acting as my referee
Bewerbung ins Blaue/Blindbewerbung	application (for a non-advertised post)
wir haben uns für X entschieden	we have chosen X for the job
jemanden einstellen	to take someone on
die leistungsgerechte Bezahlung	performance-related pay
das Monatsgehalt beträgt Euro 4000 netto	the monthly salary is 4000 euros net
die Arbeitszeit beträgt fünfunddreißig Wochenstunden	the job entails thirty-five hours per week

der Dienstwagen (-)	*company car*
durchstellen	*to put through (phone)*
die Durchwahl (en)	*extension*
die Essensmarke (n)	*meal voucher*
faxen	*to fax*
das Faxgerät (e)	*fax (machine)*
die Faxnachricht (en)	*fax (message)*
das Handy (s)	*mobile phone*
der Kopierer (-)	*copier*
der Ordner (-)	*file*
die Schreibmaschine (n)	*typewriter*
der Telefonanschluss (≈ e)	*phone connection*
das Telefongespräch (e)	*phone call*
telefonisch	*by phone*
die Telefonzentrale (n)	*switchboard*
die Unterlage (n)	*documentation*
die Vergünstigung (en)	*perk*
die Videokonferenz (en)	*video conference*
die Visitenkarte (n)	*business card*
die Voicemail (s)	*voice mail*
die Vorwahl (en)	*dialling code*
das Werbegeschenk (e)	*promotional gift*

BERUFSTÄTIG SEIN

die Abteilung (en)	*department*
die Arbeitsunfähigkeit	*unfitness for work*
die Aufgabe (n)	*job, task*
das Aufgabengebiet (e)	*area of responsibility*
die Beförderung (en)	*promotion*
der Beruf (e)	*trade, profession*
beruflich	*professional*
beschäftigen	*to employ*
der Betriebsrat (≈ e)	*works committee*
die Besprechung (en)	*meeting*
die Dienstreise (n)	*business trip*
entlassen	*to downsize*
der Erziehungsurlaub (e)	*maternity/paternity leave*
die Fahrtkosten (pl)	*travel expenses*
die Ganztagsstelle (n)	*full-time job*
das Gehalt (≈ er)	*salary*
die Gehaltserhöhung (en)	*pay rise*
der Gehaltszettel (-)	*pay slip*
die Gewerkschaft (en)	*union*

(un)befristeter Arbeitsvertrag	*(long) short term contract*
einen Vertrag unterschreiben	*to sign a contract*
einen Termin einhalten	*to meet a deadline*
einen Termin vereinbaren	*to make an appointment*
Geschäfte mit jemandem machen	*to do business with someone*
ein Gespräch führen	*to have a conversation*
X ist krankgeschrieben	*X is off sick*

die Gleichberechtigung
equal opportunities
die Gleitzeit — *flexi-time*
die Heimarbeit — *home-working*
der/die Heimarbeiter/in (-/nen)
home-worker
die Hierarchie (n) — *hierarchy*
das Homeoffice — *home office*
der Jahresbonus — *annual bonus*
das Jobsharing — *job share*
der Karrierepfad — *career path*
die Konferenz (en) — *conference*
die Kündigung (en) — *notice to quit*
das Meeting (s) — *meeting*
die Probezeit (en) — *probationary period*
das Seminar (e) — *seminar*
die Teamarbeit — *team work*
die Teilzeitarbeit — *part-time work*
die Überstunden (pl) — *overtime*
das Urlaubsgeld (er) — *holiday pay*

die Verantwortung (en) — *responsibility*
die Vollversammlung (en)
general meeting
die Zusammenarbeit — *co-operation*

MENSCHEN

der/die Arbeitgeber/in (-/nen)
employer
der/die Arbeitnehmer/in (-/nen)
employee
der/die Assistent/in (-/nen) — *assistant*
die Aushilfe (n) — *temp*
die Belegschaft (en) — *staff*
der/die Berater/in (-/nen) — *consultant*
der/die Besitzer/in (-/nen) — *owner*
der/die Buchhalter/in (-/nen)
accountant
der/die Büroangestellte (n)
office worker
die Bürokraft (⁎ e) — *office clerk*

fristgemäß kündigen — *to give notice in time*
bezahlte Urlaubstage — *paid holiday*
zur Verschwiegenheit verpflichtet — *bound to secrecy*
Weihnachtsgeld bekommen — *to get a Christmas bonus*
von zu Hause aus arbeiten — *to work from home*
den Job verlieren — *to be made redundant*
gefeuert werden — *to be sacked*
ungerechte Kündigung — *unfair dismissal*
im Ausland arbeiten — *to work abroad*
sie arbeitet freiberuflich — *she is self-employed*

der/die Chef/in (s/nen)	*boss*	der Kollege (n)	*colleague (m)*
der/die Geschäftsführer/in (-/nen)		die Kollegin (nen)	*colleague (f)*
	managing director	der Kunde (n)	*customer (m)*
die Geschäftsleitung (en)	*management*	die Kundin (nen)	*customer (f)*
die Geschäftsleute (pl)		der/die Lieferant/in (en/nen)	*supplier*
	business people	der/die Manager/in (-/nen)	*manager*
der/die Geschäftspartner/in (-/nen)		der/die Sachbearbeiter/in (-/nen)	*clerk*
	business partner	der/die Sekretär/in (-/nen)	*secretary*
der/die Gesellschafter/in (-/nen)		der/die Unternehmer/in (-/nen)	
	partner, shareholder		*entrepreneur*
der/die Gruppenleiter/in (-/nen)		der/die Vertreter/in (-/nen)	
	team leader		*representative*
der/die Inhaber/in (-/nen)	*owner*	der/die Vorgesetzte (n)	*line manager*
der/die Käufer/in (-/nen)	*purchaser*	der Vorstand	*executive board*

VOKABELTIPP

Treppenspiel (ein Spiel für zwei oder mehr Personen)

Wählen Sie einen Buchstaben. Jeder Spieler muss dann Treppen bauen.

Wer in fünf Minuten die meisten Treppen baut, gewinnt.

1. **S**
2. **so**
3. **Sie**
4. **seit**
5. **schön**
6. **Schule**
7. **Schrank**
8. **schuldig**
9. **Sammlerin**

…

Tipp! Wenn Ihre Mitspieler(innen) neue Wörter haben, schreiben Sie sie ins Vokabelheft – so erweitern Sie Ihren Wortschatz!

AUSLÄNDER

MENSCHEN

der/die Asylsuchende (n)
asylum seeker

der/die Außenseiter/in (-/nen) *outsider*

der/die Aussiedler/in (-/nen) *immigrant*
(especially from Eastern Europe)

der/die Besucher/in (-/nen) *visitor*

der/die Bürger/in (-/nen) *citizen*

der Einwanderer (-) *immigrant*

der Flüchtling (e) *refugee*

der/die Fremdarbeiter/in (-/nen)
foreign worker

der/die Gastarbeiter/in (-/nen)
immigrant worker

die Menschenhändler (pl)
human trafficking gangs

der/die politisch Verfolgte (n)
political refugee

der/die Reisende (n) *traveller*

der/die Übersiedler/in (-/nen) *migrant*

der/die Vertriebene (n) *exile*

der/die Zigeuner/in (-/nen) *gypsy*

EINWANDERUNG

die Abschiebung (en) *deportation*

sich abkapseln *to isolate yourself*

sich anpassen *to fit in*

die Arbeitsgenehmigung (en)
work permit

das Asyl *(political) asylum*

Asyl erhalten *to be granted asylum*

der Asylantrag (¨ e)
application for asylum

der/die Asylbewerber/in(-/nen)
asylum seeker

das Asylbewerberheim (e)
hostel for asylum applicants

die Gründe für die Einreise	*reasons for entry*
Anspruch auf Asyl	*right of asylum*
ethnische Herkunft	*ethnic origin*
ethnische Minderheit	*ethnic minority*
politischer Flüchtling	*political refugee*
sozialer Flüchtling	*economic refugee*
illegaler Einwanderer	*illegal immigrant*
von russischer Abstammung sein	*to be of Russian descent*

das Asylgesetz (e)	*asylum law*	die Integration	*integration*
der Asylmissbrauch (¨ e)		der/die Mitbürger/in (-/nen)	
	misuse of asylum laws		*fellow citizen*
die Aufenthaltserlaubnis (se)		das Sprachproblem (e)	
	residence permit		*language difficulty*
das Aufnahmeland (¨ er)	*host country*	die Staatsbürgerschaft	*citizenship*
der Ausreiseantrag (¨ e)		das Visum (Visen)	*visa*
	application to leave the country	der Wohnort (e)	*place of residence*
das Aussiedlerheim (e)		der Zuzug	*influx*
	immigrants hostel		
der Brauch (¨ e)	*custom*		

RASSISMUS

die Einbürgerung	*naturalisation*	aufhetzen	*to incite*
das Einbürgerungsgesetz (e)		ausländerfeindlich	*xenophobic*
	naturalisation law	der Brandanschlag (¨ e)	*arson attack*
sich einleben	*to settle down*	die Clique (n)	*group, clique*
das Herkunftsland (¨ er)		die Demonstration (en)	
	country of origin		*demonstration*

echter/falscher Anspruch (auf Einwanderung)	*genuine/bogus claim (for asylum)*
nach Deutschland eingeschmuggelt werden	*to be smuggled into Germany*
illegale Grenzübertritte	*illegal border crossings*
von einer Schlepperorganisation nach Deutschland gebracht werden	*to be brought to Germany illegally by a special organisation*
in Deutschland akzeptiert sein	*to be accepted in Germany*
Verweigerung des Menschenrechts auf Asyl	*denial of human right to asylum*
die Abschiebung abgelehnter Asylbewerber	*deportation of people denied asylum*
deutsche Staatsangehörigkeit	*German citizenship*
deutsche Staatsbürgerschaft annehmen	*to become a German national*
die multikulturelle Gesellschaft	*multicultural society*

11

die Diskriminierung (en)	*discrimination*
einschüchtern	*to intimidate*
engstirnig	*small-minded*
die Erniedrigung (en)	*humiliation*
der Fremdenhass	*hatred of foreigners*
der Gruppendruck	*group pressure*
der Kurzhaarschnitt (e)	*short haircut*
die Intoleranz	*intolerance*
der Krawall (e)	*riot, brawl*
das Motiv (e)	*motive*
der Neofaschismus	*neo-fascism*
der Neonazi (s)	*neo-nazi*
der Rassenkrawall (e)	*race riot*
der Rassismus	*racism*
der/die Rechtsextremist/in (en/nen)	*right-wing extremist*
der Rechtsradikalismus	*right-wing extremism*
der Skinhead (s)	*skinhead*
der Terror	*terror*
die Unterdrückung (en)	*suppression*
die Verfolgung (en)	*persecution*

verspotten	*to taunt*
das Vorurteil (e)	*prejudice*

ALLGEMEINES

der Akzent (e)	*accent*
der Dialekt (e)	*dialect*
einheimisch	*native*
gemischtrassig	*of mixed race*
die Großfamilie (n)	*extended family*
die Hautfarbe (n)	*skin colour*
die Herkunft (ᴗ e)	*descent, background*
die Lebensart (en)	*way of life*
die Mischehe (n)	*mixed marriage*
die Nationalität (en)	*nationality*
der Patriotismus	*patriotism*
die Rassentrennung (en)	*racial segregation*
die Tradition (en)	*tradition*
die Überfremdung	*foreign infiltration*
die Vernunftehe (n)	*marriage of convenience*
zweisprachig	*bilingual*

rassistische Spannungen	*racial tensions*
rassistisches Vorurteil	*racial prejudice*
Beziehungen zwischen den Rassen	*race relations*
rassistischer Übergriff	*racially-motivated attack*
rechtsradikales Gedankengut	*right-wing extremist ideas*
Ausschreitung gegen Ausländer	*rioting against foreigners*
Anschläge auf Asylbewerberheime	*attacks on hostels for asylum applicants*
Ausländer-raus-Parolen	*anti-foreigner slogans (foreigners out)*

sich in einem fremden Land (un)wohl fühlen	*to feel (uneasy) at ease in a foreign country*
sich wie zu Hause fühlen	*to feel at home*
die Eingliederung in die Gesellschaft	*integration into society*
andere Länder, andere Sitten	*different countries have different customs*
sich mit jemandem identifizieren	*to identify with someone*
Deutsch als Fremdsprache lernen	*to learn German as a foreign language*

VOKABELTIPP

Unbekannte Wörter

So können Sie die Bedeutung eines Wortes herausfinden:

1. Wie ist das Wort aufgebaut?
2. Sehen Sie sich den Textzusammenhang an (worum geht es im Text?).

Zum Beispiel: In einem Text über das Bankwesen finden Sie das Ihnen unbekannte Wort *Geheimzahl.*
Dieses Wort besteht aus zwei Wörtern: Geheim *(secret)* und Zahl *(number).*
Secret number im Bankwesen könnte vielleicht *PIN-number* bedeuten.
Um das festzustellen, schlagen Sie das Wort im Wörterbuch nach.

Aus welchen Teilen bestehen diese Wörter? Was bedeuten sie auf Englisch?

a) Auspuffgase – Aus *(out)* puff *(puff)* Gase *(gases)* = *exhaust fumes*
b) Arbeitgeber
c) Umweltverschmutzung
d) Taschenbuch
e) Handschuh
f) Fußgängerunterführung

Kennen Sie andere Wörter? Machen Sie eine Liste!

COMPUTER UND TECHNOLOGIE

<u>ELEKTRONISCHE DATENVERARBEITUNG UND NEUE TECHNOLOGIEN</u>

HARDWARE

der Bildschirmschoner (-)	*screensaver*
der Chip (s)	*computer chip*
der CD-Brenner (-)	*CD burner*
das CD-Laufwerk (e)	*CD drive*
die CD-ROM (s)	*CD-ROM*
die Diskette (n)	*disc*
diskettenbetriebenes System	*DOS*
das Diskettenlaufwerk	*disc drive*
der Farbdrucker (-)	*colour printer*
die Festplatte (n)	*hard drive*
der Großrechner (-)	*mainframe*
der Heimcomputer (-)	*home computer*
der Laptop (s)	*laptop*
der Laserdrucker (-)	*laser printer*
das Diskettenlaufwerk (e)	*disc drive*
das Modell (e)	*model*
das Modem (s)	*modem*
der Monitor (en)	*monitor*
das Netzwerk (e)	*network*
das Netzwerkkabel (-)	*network cable*

das Notebook (s)	*notebook*
der PC (s)	*PC*
die Plattform (en)	*platform*
der Scanner (-)	*scanner*
der Server (-)	*server*
die Speicherkapazität (en)	*memory size*
die Tastatur (en)	*keyboard*
die Taste (n)	*key*
das Terminal (-)	*terminal*
die Vernetzung (en)	*networking*
das WAP-Handy (s)	*WAP phone*
das Zubehör (-)	*accessory*

SOFTWARE

die Animation (en)	*animation*
der Backup	*back up*
die Datei (en)	*data file*
der Datenaustausch	*data exchange*
die Datenbank (en)	*database*
das Dialogfenster (-)	*pop-up window*
das Dokument (e)	*document*
die Funktionalität	*functionality*

der elektronische Organiser/Notebook	*electronic organiser/notebook*
vom Internet heruntergeladene Musikstücke auf CD brennen	*to burn a CD with music downloaded from the internet*
leerer Akku	*empty battery*
den Akku aufladen	*to recharge the battery*
eine ergonomische Maus	*an ergonomic mouse*

14

die Hilfe	*help*
das Hilfsprogramm (e)	*utility*
das Menü (s)	*menu*
das Multimedia	*multimedia*
das Programm (e)	*programme*
die Programmänderung (en)	
	programme modification
die Programmiersprache (n)	
	programming language
der Release	*release*
die Shareware	*shareware*
die Sicherungskopie (n)	*back-up copy*
der Sound (s)	*sound*
die Tabellenkalkulation (en)	
	spreadsheet
die Textverarbeitung	*word-processing*
das Update (s)	*update*
der Upgrade (s)	*upgrade*
der Virencheck	*virus check*

INTERNET

die Anlage (n)	*attachment*
der Benutzername (n)	*user ID*

die Bookmark (s)	*bookmark*
der Chatroom (s)	*chatroom*
das Cookie (s)	*cookie*
das Cybercafé (s)	*cybercafé*
der Cyberspace	*cyberspace*
die Domain-Registrierung	
	domain registration
der Doppelklick (s)	*double click*
dot	*dot*
der Download (s)	*download*
downloaden	*to download*
die Echtzeit	*realtime*
die E-Mail-Adresse	*e-mail address*
die Firewall	*firewall*
das Forum (Foren)	*forum*
die Generation @	*the e-generation*
der Hit (s)	*hit*
die Homepage	*homepage*
die HTML-Sprache	
	HTML (Hypertext Markup Language)
der Internetanschluss	
	internet connection

der neue Release ist ab Dezember verfügbar	*the new release is available from December onwards*
Software zum Download anbieten	*to offer software to be downloaded*
durch verbesserte Technik	*through improved technology*
durch technische Verbesserungen	*through technological improvements*
computerunterstütztes Lernen	*computer-aided learning*
ein anwenderfreundliches Programm	*a user-friendly programme*
grafische Benutzeroberfläche	*graphical user interface*

15

der Link (s)	*link*	das World Wide Web	*world wide web*
die Mailbox	*mailbox*	das HTTP	
online	*online*	HTTP (Hypertext Transfer Protocol)	
die Optionen (pl)	*options*		
das Passwort (⁓ er)	*password*		
das Portal (e)	*portal*		

E-COMMERCE

der Provider (-)	*provider*
der Silver Surfer (s)	*silver surfer*
die Snailmail	*snail mail*
Suche starten	*to start a search*
die Suchmaschine (n)	*search engine*
der Surfer (-)	*surfer*
die URL	
URL (Uniform Resource Locator)	
der User (-)	*user*
der (Web-)Browser (-)	*web browser*
der Webmaster (-)	*webmaster*
die Website (s)	*website*

die Anmeldegebühr (en)

registration fee

der Auktionsbeginn — *auction start time*

das Auktionsende (n)

auction end time

die Dotcom Firma	*dotcom company*
der Exchange (s)	*exchange*
der Gewinner (-)	*winner*
der Katalog (e)	*catalogue*
der Marktplatz (⁓ e)	*marketplace*
der Meistbietende (n)	*highest bidder*
die Online-Auktion (en)	*online auction*

Anzahl ändern	*to change the quantity*
Artikel anbieten	*to offer items*
Auktion eröffnen	*to start an auction*
im Internet surfen	*to surf the net*
auf einen Link klicken	*to click on a link*
virtuelle Wirklichkeit	*virtual reality*
eine Seite aktualisieren	*to update a webpage*
Infos auf einen Klick	*information at a click*
die WAP-Technologie macht das Internet mobil	*WAP technology makes the internet mobile*
mit dem Handy surfen	*to surf using a mobile phone*
mit einem WAP-fähigen Handy haben Sie ständig Zugriff auf Nachrichten	*using a WAP phone, you have constant access to news*

der Startpreis (e)	*starting price*	beenden	*to quit*
die Steigerungsstufe (n)	*bid increment*	bewegen	*to drag*
die Transaktionsgebühr	*transaction fee*	einfügen	*to paste*
die Umsatzprovision (en)		eingeben	*to enter (data)*
	sales commission	eintippen	*to key in*
verbleibende Zeit	*time left*	entwerfen	*to design*
die Versandbedingungen (pl)		entwickeln	*to develop*
	shipping conditions	initialisieren	*to initialise*
die Versandkosten (pl)		kommunizieren	*to communicate*
	post and packaging	kopieren	*to copy*
der Warenkorb (⁓ e)	*shopping cart*	laden	*to load*
der Webkatalog	*web catalogue*	personalisieren	*to personalise*
		scannen	*to scan*

FUNKTIONEN

sichern — *to save*

abmelden/anmelden	*to log off/on*
aktualisieren	*to update*
anklicken	*to click on*
anzeigen	*to display*
aufrüsten	*to upgrade*
ausdrucken	*to print out*
ausschneiden	*to cut*
bearbeiten	*to edit, revise*

übertragen — *to transmit*
verbinden — *to connect*
wiederfinden — *to retrieve*

PROBLEME

der Computergeek (s)	*computer geek*
der Crash	*crash*
die Datensicherheit	*data security*

mit dem Verkäufer Kontakt aufnehmen	*to contact the seller*
zum Warenkorb hinzufügen	*add to shopping basket*
aus dem Warenkorb herausnehmen	*remove from shopping basket*
Warenkorb anzeigen	*display shopping basket*
Peter bietet 600 Euros für einen DVD-Player	*Peter makes an offer of 600 euros for a DVD player*
Angebot der Woche	*this week's special*
weiter einkaufen	*continue shopping*
akzeptierte Zahlungsmittel	*accepted methods of payment*

der/die Hacker/in (-/nen)	*hacker*
harter/weicher Porno	*hard/soft porn*
die Kompatibilität	*compatibility*
die Pornografie	*pornography*
pornografisch	*pornographic*
der Programmfehler (-)	*bug*
die Raubkopie (n)	*pirate copy*
die Software-Piraterie	*software piracy*
der Systemfehler (-)	*system error*
verbreiten	*to disseminate*
der Virus (Viren)	*virus*
die Zensur (en)	*censorship*

TECHNOLOGIE

anpassen	*to adapt*
der Astronaut (en)	*astronaut*
die Crew	*crew*
fernsteuern	*to remote control*
die NASA	*NASA*
die Rakete (n)	*rocket*
die Raumfähre (n)/das Raumschiff (e)	*space shuttle*
die Raumstation/Weltraumstation (en)	*space station*

eine Webseite entwerfen	*to design a webpage*
sich ans Internet anmelden	*to connect to the internet*
Informationsaustausch mit Leuten aus aller Welt	*to exchange information with people around the world*
Infos tauschen	*to exchange information*
Bilder einscannen	*to scan pictures in*
Software entwickeln	*to develop software*
neue Programme installieren	*to install new computer programmes*
Datenkopien erstellen	*to back up*
Fehler suchen	*to de-bug*

die Kluft zwischen Computererfahrenen und -unerfahrenen	*the digital divide*
Kinder stehen in der Gefahr, computersüchtig zu werden	*children are in danger of becoming addicted to computers*
pornografische Materialien downloaden	*to download pornographic material*
das Internet benutzen, um Informationen zu verbreiten	*to use the internet to disseminate information*

18

der Roboter (-)	*robot*	die Schwerelosigkeit	*weightlessness*
der Satellit (en)	*satellite*	das Weltall	*outer space*

der Flug zum Mond	*visit to the moon*
einen Satelliten in eine Umlaufbahn bringen	*to put a satellite into orbit*
ein Spaziergang im All	*a space walk*
ins All	*into space*
außerirdische Lebensformen	*extraterrestrial life forms*
eine sichere Marslandung	*safe landing on Mars*
bemannter Raumflug zum Mars	*human mission to Mars*
Experimente durchführen	*to carry out experiments*
wissenschaftliche Fortschritte	*scientific advances*
die Satellitenkommunikation	*satellite communications*
wissenschaftlicher Wert	*scientific value*

VOKABELTIPP

Das ABC-Adjektivspiel (ein Spiel für zwei oder mehr Personen)
Adjektive sind sehr nützlich, wenn Sie einen Aufsatz oder eine Geschichte lebendiger machen wollen. Wie viele Adjektive kennen Sie schon? Versuchen Sie dieses Spiel. Gehen Sie das Alphabet durch. Wer kein Adjektiv einfügen kann, scheidet aus.

A: Meine Katze ist eine **a**dlige Katze.
B: Meine Katze ist eine **b**erufstätige Katze.
C: Meine Katze ist eine **c**haotische Katze …

Tipp! Wenn Ihre Mitspieler(innen) neue Adjektive finden, schreiben Sie sie ins Vokabelheft – so erweitern Sie Ihren Wortschatz!

Alternative Sätze:
Mein Hund ist ein … er Hund.
Mein Kaninchen ist ein … es Kaninchen.
Meine Meerschweinchen sind … e Meerschweinchen.

DEUTSCHLAND

POLITIK

der/die Abgeordnete (n)
member of parliament

abwählen — *to vote out of office*

das Amt (⸚ er) — *office*

die Außenpolitik — *foreign policy*

der Ausschuss (⸚ e) — *committee*

der Beamte (n) — *civil servant (m)*

die Beamtin (nen) — *civil servant (f)*

die Behörde (n) — *authority*

das Bundesland (⸚ er) — *federal state*

auf Bundesebene — *at a national level*

der Bundeskanzler (-)
federal chancellor

der Bundestag — *federal parliament*

der Bundesrat — *Bundesrat*
(upper house of German parliament)

die Bundesregierung (en)
federal government

der/die Bürger/in (-/nen) — *citizen*

demokratisch — *democratic*

der Erdrutschsieg (e) — *landslide victory*

die Erststimme (n) — *first vote*

die Faktion (en) — *party, faction*

föderalistisch — *federal*

gesetzgebend — *legislative*

das Gipfeltreffen (-) — *summit meeting*

die Grundordnung (en) — *basic order*

das Grundrecht (e) — *basic right*

die Interessengemeinschaft (en)
pressure group

das Kabinett (e) — *cabinet*

der Kapitalismus — *capitalism*

die Koalition (en) — *coalition*

die Bundesrepublik Deutschland (BRD)	*Federal Republic of Germany (FRG)*
die Deutsche Demokratische Republik (DDR)	*German Democratic Republic (GDR)*
Christlich-Demokratische Union (CDU)	*Christian Democratic Union*
Freie Demokratische Partei (F.D.P.)	*Free Democratic Party*
die Grünen	*Green Party*
Nationalsozialistische Partei Deutschlands (NPD)	*National Socialist Party of Germany*
die Republikaner	*Republican Party*
Sozialdemokratische Partei Deutschlands (SPD)	*Social Democratic Party of Germany*

die Landesregierung (en)
regional government

der Landtag (e) *regional parliament*

das Manifest *manifesto*

die Mehrheit (en) *majority*

das Mehrparteiensystem
multi-party system

die Menschenrechte (pl) *human rights*

die Opposition (en) *opposition*

die Partei (en) *party*

die Parlamentssitzung (en)
parliamentary session

das Parteimitglied (er) *party member*

politisch korrekt *politically correct*

die Ratifizierung (en) *ratification*

die Regierung (en) *government*

der Rücktritt (e) *resignation*

der/die Spitzenkandidat/in (en/nen)
top candidate

der/die Staatspräsident/in (en/nen)
the president

die Stimme (n) *vote*

die Verfassung (en) *constitution*

verfassungsgemäß *constitutional*

die Versammlung (en) *assembly*

die Verwaltung (en) *administration*

die Volksabstimmung (en) *plebiscite*

der Volksentscheid (e) *referendum*

die Vorschrift (en) *regulation*

die Wahl (en) *vote, election*

wahlberechtigt *entitled to vote*

das Wahlergebnis (se) *election result*

die Wählerschaft (en) *electorate*

der Wahlkampf (⸚ e)
election campaign

der Wahlkreis (e) *constituency*

die Wahlurne (n) *ballot box*

die Weltanschauung (en) *world view*

die Zweitstimme (n) *second vote*

EHEMALIGE DDR

die Abgrenzung (en) *separation*

antifaschistisch *anti-fascist*

eine absolute Mehrheit bekommen	*to get an absolute majority*
auf der politischen Tagesordnung stehen	*to be on the political agenda*
mit der Politik einverstanden sein	*to agree with the politics*
eine solide politische Grundlage	*a solid political foundation*
zum Kompromiss bereit sein	*to be prepared to compromise*
Aufruf zum politischen Soforteingriff	*to call for urgent government action*
der politische Gegner	*political opponent*
das Scheitern der Verhandlungen	*breakdown of talks*
der Sturz der Regierung	*the downfall of the government*
eine krachende Niederlage	*a crashing defeat*

die Arbeiterbewegung (en)
labour movement

die Arbeiterklasse (n)   *working class*

der Aufstand (⁓ e)   *revolt*

das Ausreisevisum (-sen)   *exit visa*

die (Berliner) Mauer   *the (Berlin) Wall*

die DDR-Gründung
founding of the GDR

der DDRler   *person from the GDR*

der Diktator (en)   *dictator*

die Einheit (en)   *unity*

der Eiserne Vorhang   *the Iron Curtain*

die Entnazifizierung   *denazification*

die Genossenschaft (en)   *co-operative*

der Grenzübergang (⁓ e)
border crossing

der Kalte Krieg   *the Cold War*

kollektiv   *collective*

der Kommunismus   *communism*

die Nationalisierung   *nationalisation*

der Ossi (s) (inf) *east German (person)*

der Ostblock   *Eastern bloc*

Ostdeutschland
East Germany (since unification)

die Pleitewirtschaft (en)
bankrupt economy

das Politbüro   *Politburo*

der Proletarier (-)   *proletarian*

die Reisefreiheit (en) *freedom to travel*

der Sozialismus   *socialism*

die Spionage   *spying*

die Staatssicherheit (Stasi)
state security service

die Stasi-Akten (pl)   *state security files*

die Stasi-Herrschaft   *state security rule*

die Trennung (en)   *division*

die Treuhand   *privatisation agency*

der Umbruch (⁓ e)   *radical change*

die Verbitterung   *bitterness*

die Vereinigung   *unification*

volkseigen   *nationally owned*

die Volkskammer   *GDR parliament*

der Warschauer Pakt   *Warsaw pact*

der/die Werktätige (n)   *worker*

der Fall der Mauer   *falling of the Berlin Wall*

Tag der deutschen Einheit (3. Oktober)   *German unification day (3rd October)*

die Flut nach Westen   *flood to the west*

die Verlegung des Regierungssitzes von Bonn nach Berlin   *transfer of the seat of government from Bonn to Berlin*

Steuererhöhungen zur Finanzierung der Einheit   *the tax increases to finance unification*

jeder dritte Arbeitsplatz in der DDR ist wegrationalisiert worden   *every third job in the GDR was cut*

Sorgen um die wirtschaftliche und soziale Existenz   *worries about financial and social livelihood*

der Wessi (s) (inf) *west German (person)*
der Wiederaufbau *reconstruction*
der Wohlstand *affluence*
zusammenwachsen *to grow together*

NAZIZEIT

die Alliierten (pl) *allies*
der Anschluss (-̈ e) *annexation*
arisch *Aryan*
die Besatzungsmacht (-̈ e) *occupying force*
die Besatzungszone (n) *occupation zone*
der Blitzkrieg *blitzkrieg*
die Braunhemden (pl) *Brownshirts*
die Bücherverbrennung (en) *book burning*

Drittes Reich *Third Reich*
die Endlösung *final solution*
der Faschismus *fascism*
der Führer (-) *leader, Hitler*
die Gaskammer (n) *gas chamber*
die Gestapo *gestapo*
das Getto (s) *ghetto*
das Hakenkreuz (e) *swastika*
die Hitlerjugend *Hitler youth*
der Holocaust (s) *Holocaust*
der/die Holocaustüberlebende (n) *holocaust survivor*
der Kriegsverbrecher (-) *war criminal*
die Kristallnacht *night of the breaking glass*
der Jude (n) *Jew (m)*
die Jüdin (nen) *Jew (f)*
der Judenhass *anti-Semitism*

nach Kriegsende wurde Berlin in vier Sektoren geteilt *after the war Berlin was divided into four sectors*
die Alliierten übten die Staatsgewalt aus *the Allies assumed control*
Berlin (Ost) wurde 1968 zur Hauptstadt der DDR erklärt *in 1968 Berlin (East) was declared the capital of the GDR*
die gewaltsame Trennung der Familien und Freunde *the forced separation of families and friends*
der radikale Wechsel vom Alten zum Neuen *radical change from old to new*
Wunden hinterlassen *to leave scars*
die Folgen des Zweiten Weltkrieges *the consequences of the Second World War*
für Kriegsverbrechen angeklagt sein *to be indicted of war crimes*
gezwungen sein, sich zu verstecken *to be forced into hiding*
Widerstand leisten *to offer resistance*

die Judenverfolgung (en)
persecution of the Jews

die Kapitulation   *capitulation*

das Konzentrationslager (-)
concentration camp

der Kriegsausbruch   *outbreak of war*

die Luftwaffe   *the Luftwaffe*

der Nationalsozialismus
national socialism

der/das Pogrom (e)   *pogrom*

die Propagandamaschine
propaganda machine

der Putsch (e)   *coup*

die Vernichtung (en)   *extermination*

das Vernichtungslager (-)
extermination camp

die West-/Ostfront
the West/East Front

der Widerstand   *resistance*

die Wiedergutmachung   *compensation*

VOKABELTIPP

Abkürzungen

Beim Lesen oder im Fernsehen stoßen Sie oft auf Abkürzungen.

Jedes Bundesland in Deutschland hat eine Abkürzung, die häufig gebraucht wird:

BW	Baden-Württemberg	NI	Niedersachsen
BY	Bayern	NW	Nordrhein-Westfalen
BE	Berlin	RP	Rheinland-Pfalz
BB	Brandenburg	SL	Saarland
HB	Bremen	SN	Sachsen
HH	Hamburg	ST	Sachsen-Anhalt
HE	Hessen	SH	Schleswig-Holstein
MV	Mecklenburg-Vorpommern	TH	Thüringen

Auch andere Phrasen und Redewendungen werden abgekürzt.

Was bedeuten folgende Abkürzungen?

z.B.   z.H.   usw.   Pkw   v.a.   d.h.   u.v.a.   bzw.   u.ä.

FREIZEIT

SPORT

der/die Anhänger/in (-/nen) *supporter*

die Anstrengung (en) *exertion*

die Ausdauer *stamina*

der/die Berufssportler/in (-/nen)

professional sportsperson

die Bewegung (en) *exercise, movement*

die Bundesliga *German national league*

das Doping *drug-taking*

das Endspiel (e) *final*

die Europameisterschaft (en)

European championship

der Fan (s) *fan*

der/die Finalist/in (en/nen) *finalist*

das Foulspiel *foul play*

der Fußballrowdy (s) *football hooligan*

der/die Gegner/in (-/nen) *opponent*

das Halbfinale (-finalspiele) *semi-final*

der Klub (s) *club*

die Leistung (en) *achievement*

der Leistungssport (arten)

competitive sport

der/die Manager/in (-/nen) *manager*

die Mannschaft (en) *team*

das Mannschaftsspiel (e) *team game*

der/die Medaillengewinner/in (-/nen)

medallist

der/die Meister/in (-/nen) *champion*

die Meisterschaft (en) *championship*

die Muskelpille (n) *muscle pill*

der/die Nationalspieler/in (-/nen)

national player

die Niederlage (n) *defeat*

die Olympiade *Olympics*

der/die Olympiasieger/in (-/nen)

olympic champion

der Pokal (e) *cup*

das Preisgeld (er) *prize money*

der Profi (s) *pro*

der Publikumssport *spectator sport*

die Rangliste (n) *ranking*

dein Land repräsentieren	*to represent your country*
bis zu fünf Stunden am Tag trainieren	*to train for up to five hours a day*
einen Rekord brechen	*to break a record*
der Kampf um den Titel	*the fight for the title*
die Olympischen Spiele	*the Olympic Games*
ein Match festlegen	*to fix a match*

der/die Rekordhalter/in (-/nen)	*record-holder*
die Rennbahn (en)	*race track*
die Saison (s)	*season*
schlagen	*to beat, hit*
der Sieg (e)	*victory*
das Sitzplatzstadion (-ien)	*all-seater stadium*
das Spielfeld (er)	*playing area*
die Spielregel (n)	*rule*
die Spielzeit (en)	*playing time*
der/die Spitzensportler/in (-/nen)	*top-class sportsperson*
der/die Sponsor/in (en/nen)	*sponsor*
die Sportart (en)	*type of sport*
teilnehmen	*to take part*
der/die Teilnehmer/in (-/nen)	*participant*
der/die Trainer/in (-/nen)	*coach*
das Trainingslager (-)	*training camp*
die Transfersumme (n)	*transfer fee*
das Turnier (e)	*tournament*
unschlagbar	*unbeatable*
der Verteidiger (-)	*defender*

der/die Weltmeister/in (-/nen)	*world champion*
die Weltmeisterschaft (en)	*world championship*
die Weltrangliste (n)	*world listing*
der Weltrekord (e)	*world record*
wetten	*to bet*
der Wettkampf (⸚ e)	*competition*
der/die Zuschauer/in (-/nen)	*spectator*

REISEN

abenteuerlich	*adventurous*
die Abreise (n)	*departure*
der Aufenthalt (e)	*stay*
die Besichtigung (en)	*visit*
der Charterflug (⸚ e)	*charter flight*
entdecken	*to discover*
die Eintrittskarte (n)	*entrance ticket*
die Entfernung (en)	*distance*
sich erholen	*to recover, recuperate*
das Faulenzen	*lazing around*
der Ferienort (e)	*holiday resort*
die Ferienwohnung (en)	*holiday flat*
der Fernflug (⸚ e)	*longhaul flight*

der Drogenzufallstest	*random drugs-testing*
einen Dopingtest machen	*to take a drugs test*
die Dopingkontrolle ist positiv	*the drugs test is positive*
die leistungsfördernden Drogen (pl)	*performance-enhancing drugs*
die verbotenen Substanzen (pl)	*banned substances*
die Gewaltbereitschaft beim Fußball	*football violence*

die Flughafensteuer (n) *airport tax*

die Flugverspätungen (pl)

airport delays

der Fremdenverkehr *tourism*

die Gruppenreise (n) *group holiday*

die Hauptsaison (s) *high season*

die Impfung (en) *vaccination*

der Linienflug (= e) *scheduled flight*

die Pauschalreise (n) *package holiday*

der Reiseboom (s) *travel boom*

das Reisebüro (s) *travel agency*

der/die Reiseleiter/in (-/nen)

tour leader

die Reiseplanung (en) *travel plans*

der Reiseprospekt (e) *travel brochure*

die Reiseroute (n) *itinerary*

das Reiseziel (e) *destination*

der Rucksackurlaub (e)

backpacking trip

die Rundreise (n) *round trip*

sehenswert *worth visiting*

die Sehenswürdigkeiten (pl) *sights*

die Städtetour (en) *city tour*

der Strandurlaub (e) *beach holiday*

der Tagesausflug (= e) *day trip*

die Tour (en) *outing, trip*

die Tourismusbranche (n)

tourist industry

das Touristenzentrum (-zentren)

tourist centre

trampen *to hitch hike*

der Traumurlaub (e) *dream holiday*

urlaubsreif *ready for a holiday*

die Urlaubszeit (en) *holiday time*

die Unterkunft (= e) *accommodation*

unterwegs sein *to be travelling*

das Verkehrsamt (= er) *tourist office*

verreisen *to go away (on holiday)*

weltberühmt *world famous*

die Weltreise (n) *world trip*

der Zuschlag (= e) *supplement*

FEIERTAGE

Diese gesetzlichen Feiertage sind
von Bundesland zu Bundesland
verschieden.

Neujahr (1.1.) *New Year*

Heilige Drei Könige (6.1.) *Epiphany*

Karfreitag *Good Friday*

Ostersonntag *Easter Sunday*

etwa 1,5 Millionen Arbeitsplätze hängen von der Tourismusnachfrage ab
about 1.5 million jobs rely on the demand from tourists

einen Urlaub online buchen
to book a holiday on the internet

man kann das Land das ganze Jahr über bereisen
you can visit the country at any time of year

sich die Stadt auf eigene Faust ansehen
to visit the town on your own

Ostermontag	*Easter Monday*
Maifeiertag/Tag der Arbeit (1.5.)	
	May Day
Christi Himmelfahrt	*Ascension*
Pfingstsonntag	*Whitsun*
Pfingstmontag	*Whit Monday*
Fronleichnam	*Corpus Christi*
Mariä Himmelfahrt (15.8.)	
	Assumption
Tag der deutschen Einheit (3.10.)	
	German Unification Day
Erntedanktag	*Harvest Festival*
Allerheiligen (1.11.)	*All Saints' Day*
Volkstrauertag	*Remembrance Day*
Buß- und Bettag	
	Day of Prayer and Repentance

Totensonntag	*Sunday before Advent*
1. Weihnachtstag (25.12.)	
	Christmas Day
2. Weihnachtstag (26.12.)	*Boxing Day*

Weitere besondere Tage:

Valentinstag (14.2.)	*Valentine's Day*
Fastnacht/Fasching/Karneval	
	Carnival
Aschermittwoch	*Ash Wednesday*
Gründonnerstag	*Maundy Thursday*
Reformationstag (31.10.)	
	Reformation Day
Nikolaus (6.12.)	*St Nicholas*
Heiligabend (24.12.)	*Christmas Eve*
Silvester (31.12.)	*New Year's Eve*

die Zeitumstellung überwinden	*to overcome jetlag*
der/die Rucksackreisende/ der Weltenbummler	*independent traveller*
im Ausland	*abroad*
ins Ausland fahren	*to travel abroad*
Hotels verlangen sehr hohe Preise	*hotels charge very high prices*
sie ist vierzehn Tage vereist	*she has been away for a fortnight*

VOKABELTIPP

Wörterbuch: Deutsch/Englisch

Wenn Sie die Bedeutung eines deutschen Wortes oder Informationen über ein deutsches Wort suchen, schlagen Sie das Wort im Wörterbuch nach. Sie müssen aber aufpassen – einige Wörter haben mehrere Bedeutungen.

Sehen Sie diesen Auszug an und beantworten Sie die unten stehenden Fragen.

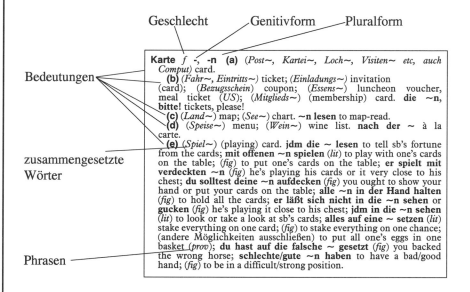

Geschlecht   Genitivform   Pluralform

Bedeutungen

zusammengesetzte Wörter

Phrasen

Karte *f* -, **-n** **(a)** (*Post~, Kartei~, Loch~, Visiten~ etc, auch Comput*) card.
(b) (*Fahr~, Eintritts~*) ticket; (*Einladungs~*) invitation (card); (*Bezugsschein*) coupon; (*Essens~*) luncheon voucher, meal ticket (*US*); (*Mitglieds~*) (membership) card. **die ~n, bitte!** tickets, please!
(c) (*Land~*) map; (*See~*) chart. **~n lesen** to map-read.
(d) (*Speise~*) menu; (*Wein~*) wine list. **nach der ~** à la carte.
(e) (*Spiel~*) (playing) card. **jdm die ~ lesen** to tell sb's fortune from the cards; **mit offenen ~n spielen** (*lit*) to play with one's cards on the table; (*fig*) to put one's cards on the table; **er spielt mit verdeckten ~n** (*fig*) he's playing his cards or it very close to his chest; **du solltest deine ~n aufdecken** (*fig*) you ought to show your hand or put your cards on the table; **alle ~n in der Hand halten** (*fig*) to hold all the cards; **er läßt sich nicht in die ~n sehen** or **gucken** (*fig*) he's playing it close to his chest; **jdm in die ~n sehen** (*lit*) to look or take a look at sb's cards; **alles auf eine ~ setzen** (*lit*) stake everything on one card; (*fig*) to stake everything on one chance; (andere Möglichkeiten ausschließen) to put all one's eggs in one basket (*prov*); **du hast auf die falsche ~ gesetzt** (*fig*) you backed the wrong horse; **schlechte/gute ~n haben** to have a bad/good hand; (*fig*) to be in a difficult/strong position.

a) Wie heißt die Pluralform von *Karte*?

b) Wie viele Hauptbedeutungen hat *Karte* auf Englisch?

c) Was ist richtig: *der/die/das Karte*?

d) Wie heißt *Weinkarte* auf Englisch?

e) Wie sagt man *Er hat mir die Karten gelesen* auf Englisch?

f) Wie sagt man *Sie deckte ihre Karten auf* auf Englisch?

GESUNDHEIT

RAUCHEN

asozial	*antisocial*
aufhören	*to give up*
inhalieren	*to inhale*
der Kehlkopfkrebs	*throat cancer*
kettenrauchen	*to chain smoke*
der Lungenkrebs	*lung cancer*
das Nikotin	*nicotine*
nikotinarm	*low-nicotine*
das Nikotinpflaster (-)	*nicotine patch*
paffen	*to puff*
die Pfeife (n)	*pipe*
der Qualm	*thick smoke*
das Rauchen	*smoking*
der/die Raucher/in (-/nen)	*smoker*
der Raucherhusten	*smoker's cough*
der Teer	*tar*
die Zigarette (n)	*cigarette*
die Zigarre (n)	*cigar*

die Zigarettenwerbung (en)	*cigarette advert*
der Zug (⁓ e)	*drag*

DROGEN

die Abhängigkeit (en)	*addiction*
die Antidrogenkampagne	*anti-drugs campaign*
clean bleiben	*to stay clean*
der Dealer (-)	*drug dealer*
die Designerdrogen (pl)	*designer drugs*
die Dosierung (en)	*dose*
der/die Drogenabhängige (n)	*drug addict*
der Drogenbaron	*drug baron*
die Drogenberatungsstelle (n)	*drug advice centre*
drogengefährdet	*at risk from drugs*

sich das Rauchen abgewöhnen	*to give up smoking*
das Rauchen verbieten	*to ban smoking*
das Rauchen gefährdet die Gesundheit	*smoking damages your health*
zehn Zigaretten pro Tag rauchen	*to smoke ten cigarettes a day*
starker Raucher sein	*to be a heavy smoker*
nach Rauch stinken	*to smell of smoke*
die Stube ist voll gequalmt/verraucht	*the room is full of smoke*
eine schwache Persönlichkeit haben	*to have an addictive personality*
Hemmungen verlieren	*to blow away inhibitions*

der Drogenhandel	*drug trafficking*	high sein	*to be high*
Drogen handeln	*to push drugs*	die Infektionsgefahr (en)	
der Drogenkonsum	*drug taking*		*risk of infection*
der/die Drogenkonsument/in (en/nen)		intravenös	*intravenous*
	drug taker	das Kokain	*cocaine*
der Drogenmissbrauch	*drug abuse*	die Legalisierung	*legalisation*
der Drogenrausch (ᴗ e)	*high on drugs*	das Rauschgift (e)	*drug*
das Ecstasy	*ecstasy*	der/die Rauschgifthändler/in (-/nen)	
der Entzug	*withdrawal from drugs*		*drug dealer*
die Entzugsanstalt (ᴗ e)		schlucken	*to swallow*
	rehabilitation centre	der/die Schnüffler/in (-/nen)	*sniffer*
die Entzugserscheinungen (pl)		schnupfen	*to snort*
	withdrawal symptoms	der Schuss (ᴗ e)	*shot*
der Fixer (-)	*junkie*	die Spritze (n)	*syringe*
das Gras	*grass*	spritzen	*to inject*
die Halluzination (en)	*hallucination*	die Sucht (ᴗ e)	*addiction*
das Haschisch	*hashish*	süchtig	*addicted*
das Heroin	*heroin*	die Überdosis (-dosen)	*overdose*
die Heroinsucht	*heroin addiction*	die Wirkung (en)	*effect*

Drogen legalisieren	*legalisation of drugs*
aus medizinischen Gründen Cannabis nehmen	*to take cannabis for medicinal purposes*
den Frust mit . . . betäuben	*to numb frustrations with . . .*
die Persönlichkeit verändern	*to change your personality*
Schadstoffe, die in den Körper geraten	*harmful substances which get into the body*
im Haschischrausch	*under the effect of hashish*
das Einnehmen von Drogen	*drug-taking*
Alleskleber schnüffeln	*to sniff glue*
einen Joint reinziehen (inf)	*to smoke a joint*
an der Nadel hängen (inf)	*to be a druggie*

31

ALKOHOL

alkoholfrei	*non-alcoholic*
der/die Alkoholiker/in (-/nen)	*alcoholic*
die Alkoholvergiftung	*alcohol poisoning*
alkoholsüchtig	*addicted to alcohol*
besoffen (inf)	*stoned, smashed*
betrunken	*drunk*
der Kater (-) (inf)	*hangover*
runterkippen (inf)	*to down*
die Kneipentour (en)	*pub crawl*
nüchtern	*sober*
der Rausch (⁀ e)	*inebriation*
saufen	*to booze*
der/die Säufer/in (-/nen)	*drunkard*
die Schankgesetze (pl)	*licensing laws*

die Spirituosen (pl)	*spirits*
sich übergeben	*to be sick*

AIDS

der/die AIDS-Kranke (n)	*AIDS sufferer*
die AIDS-Station (en)	*AIDS ward*
der AIDS-Test (s)	*AIDS test*
anstecken	*to infect*
der Ausbruch (⁀ e)	*outbreak*
die Blutbank (en)	*blood bank*
der Bluter (-)	*haemophiliac*
die Bluterkrankheit	*haemophilia*
das Blutpräparat (e)	*blood preparation*
die Blutprobe (n)	*blood test*
der Blutspender (-)	*blood donor*

minderjähriges Trinken	*under-age drinking*
unter Alkoholeinfluss	*under the influence of alcohol*
Betrunkenheit und unzweckmäßiges Benehmen	*drunk and disorderly behaviour*
Alkohol am Steuer vermeiden	*don't drink and drive*
0,8 Promille Alkohol im Blut	*0.8 ml alcohol in blood*
jemanden zum Alkohol treiben	*to drive somebody to drink*
trockener Alkoholiker sein	*to be a recovering alcoholic*
geschützter Geschlechtsverkehr	*safe sex*
HIV-verseuchte Blutkonserven	*HIV contaminated blood supplies*
sich mit HIV infizieren	*to contract HIV*
am Virus erkranken	*to contract the virus*
den Virus auf den/die Intimpartner/in übertragen	*to pass the virus on to a sexual partner*
an AIDS sterben	*to die of AIDS*

die Bluttransfusion (en)

blood transfusion

die HIV-Antikörper (pl) *HIV antibodies*

die HIV-Infektion (en)   *HIV infection*

HIV-infiziert   *infected with HIV*

HIV-kontaminiert   *HIV contaminated*

HIV-positiv   *HIV positive*

die Immunschwäche (n)

immune deficiency

das Kondom (e)   *condom*

die Prävention   *prevention*

ABTREIBUNG

die Behinderung (en)   *disability*

die Beratung (en)   *counselling*

die Beratungspflicht (en)

compulsory counselling

der Embryo (nen)   *embryo*

die Frauenklinik (en)   *women's clinic*

der Schwangerschaftsabbruch (⁓ e)

termination of pregnancy

(nicht) strafbar   *(not) punishable*

die Vergewaltigung (en)   *rape*

GESUND LEBEN

das Abendbrot   *(light) supper*

abnehmen   *to lose weight*

der Appetit   *appetite*

die Ballaststoffe (pl)   *roughage*

dick machend   *fattening*

essbar   *edible*

der Farbstoff (e)   *artificial colouring*

das Fertiggericht (e) *ready-made meal*

die Fitness   *physical fitness*

die Gastronomie   *gastronomy*

der Geschmack (⁓ e)   *taste*

das Gericht (e)   *dish*

gesüßt   *sweetened*

schwangere Minderjährige   *teenage pregnancy*

eine ungewollte Schwangerschaft *unwanted pregnancy*

Gründe für den Abbruch   *reasons for termination*

die qualifizierte Beratung der Schwangeren *qualified counselling of the pregnant woman*

die Indikationslösung (en)   *abortion on ethical, eugenic, medical or social grounds*

die Fristenregelung (en)   *law allowing termination of pregnancy within first three months*

illegale Abtreibung   *back-street abortion*

der Schutz des ungeborenen Lebens *protection of unborn life*

der/die Gegner/in der Abtreibung *anti-abortion campaigner*

33

das Getränk (e)	*drink*	organisch	*organic*
das Getreide	*grains*	pflanzliches Fett	*vegetable fat*
das Grundnahrungsmittel (-)		die Rohkost	*raw fruit/vegetables*
	basic food stuff	das Schnellrestaurant (s)	
das Hauptgericht (e)	*main course*		*fast food restaurant*
die Kalorie (n)	*calorie*	der Süßstoff (e)	*sweetener*
der Kaloriengehalt	*calorific value*	tierisches Fett	*animal fat*
das Kohlehydrat (e)	*carbohydrate*	ultra hocherhitzt	*UHT*
die Lebensmittel (pl)	*food stuffs*	der/die Vegetarier/in (-/nen)	*vegetarian*
der Leckerbissen (-)	*titbit*	vegetarisch essen	
die Mahlzeit (en)	*meal*		*to eat vegetarian food*
nahrhaft	*nourishing*	verkocht	*overcooked*
die Nahrung	*food*	das Vitamin (e)	*vitamin*
der Nährwert (e)	*nutritional value*	zunehmen	*to put on weight*
die Nascherei (en)	*nibbling*	der Zusatz (¨ e)	*additive*
der Naturkostladen (¨)		die Zutat (en)	*ingredient*
	health food shop	die Zwischenmahlzeit (en)	*snack*

die deutsche Küche	*German cuisine*
genetisch manipulierte Organismen (GMO)	*genetically modified organisms*
Produkte mit veränderten Genen	*genetically modified products*
genetisch veränderte Nahrung	*genetically modified food*
Fruchtsaft ist reich an . . .	*fruit juice is rich in . . .*
einen geringen Nährwert haben	*to have a low nutritional value*
eine ausgewogene Ernährung	*a balanced diet*
das Cholesterin im Blut erhöhen	*to raise cholesterol levels in your blood*
gute Kondition haben	*to be fit*
frisches Obst/Gemüse	*fresh fruit/vegetables*
durch eine schlechte Ernährung verursacht	*caused by a poor nutritional diet*
hast du Junkfood zu Hause?	*do you have any junkfood at home?*
ich stehe auf Fastfood (inf)	*I love fast-food*

IM KRANKENHAUS

die Allergie (n)	*allergy*
ansteckend	*infectious*
die Behandlung (en)	*treatment*
die Bluttransfusion (en)	*blood transfer*
der Blutzuckerspiegel (-)	*blood-sugar level*
bösartig	*malignant*
die Entzündung (en)	*inflammation*
die Fettleibigkeit	*obesity*
die Gesundheitsprobleme (pl)	*healthcare problems*
das Gewichtsproblem (e)	*weight problem*
gutartig	*benign*
heilen	*to cure*
die Heilkunde	*medicine*
der Herzanfall (⸚ e)	*heart attack*
das Immunsystem (e)	*immune system*
die Impfung (en)	*vaccination*
die Intensivpflege	*intensive care*
die Krankenkasse (n)	*health insurance company*
die Krankenversicherung (en)	*medical insurance*
der Krebs	*cancer*
die Kreislaufprobleme (pl)	*circulation problems*
kurzsichtig	*shortsighted*
leiden (an)	*to suffer (from)*
mimosenhaft	*oversensitive*
die Nebenwirkung (en)	*side effect*
der Organspendeausweis	*donor card*
röntgen	*to x-ray*
die Bulimie	*bulimia*
die Schönheitschirurgie	*plastic surgery*
der Stress	*stress*
der Tumor (en)	*tumour*
der Ultraschall (e)	*scan*
die Untersuchung (en)	*examination*
die Verpflanzung (en)	*transplant*
die Warteliste (n)	*waiting list*
weitsichtig	*longsighted*

landesweiter Appell für ein Organ	*a nationwide appeal for an organ*
der Mangel an Pflegebetten	*bed shortages*
in Kur gehen	*to go to a spa/health resort*
jemanden an einen Spezialisten verweisen	*to refer someone to a specialist*
sich von einer Operation erholen	*to recover from an operation*
hohen Blutdruck haben	*to have high blood pressure*
immun gegen	*immune from*
allergisch gegen	*allergic to*

ALTERNATIVE MEDIZIN

die Akupunktur	*acupuncture*
die Aromatherapie	*aromatherapy*
die Eheberatung	*marriage guidance counselling*
die Familientherapie	*family counselling*
die Fußreflexzonentherapie	*reflexology*
die Homeopathie	*homeopathy*
die Hypnose	*hypnosis*
die Massage	*massage*
die Meditation	*meditation*
die Therapie	*counselling*
in Therapie sein	*to have therapy*

der Psychologe/die Psychologin	*psychologist*
Yoga machen	*to do yoga*

MEDIZINISCHE ETHIK

die DNA	*DNA*
ethisch	*ethical*
das Gen (e)	*gene*
die Genetik	*genetics*
der/die Genforscher/in (-/nen)	*geneticist*
die Genforschung	*genetic engineering*
das Genomprojekt	*the genome project*
klonen	*to clone*
unethisch	*unethical*
die Verhaltensethik	*ethical code of conduct*

zur Ruhe kommen	*to relax*
die Ruhe bewahren	*to maintain calm*
Probleme bewältigen	*to overcome problems*
sich entspannen durch Massage	*to relax through massage*
eine Ehe retten	*to save a marriage*
das Gleichgewicht verlieren	*to lose your sense of balance*
mit sich selbst im Reinen sein	*to be in tune with yourself*
tierische Organe für die menschliche Transplantation entwickeln	*to develop animal organs for human transplant*
das Klonen menschlicher Embryonen	*cloning of human embryos*
das Gen für X entdecken	*to identify the gene for X*
der medizinische Fortschritt	*medical progress*
Erforschung der möglichen Folgen von Genmanipulationen	*research into the possible consequences of gene manipulation*
angeblich zu wissenschaftlichen Zwecken	*for supposedly scientific purposes*

Zusammengesetzte Wörter (1)

Um ein zusammengesetztes Wort zu bilden, kann man nicht immer einfach zwei Wörter zusammenschreiben. Oft kommen Buchstaben dazwischen.

das Meer + es + die Früchte = die Meeresfrüchte

Wie setzt man diese Wörter zusammen?

a) Mitte + Nacht = die Mitternacht (midnight)

b) Tag + Anbruch

c) Geschäft + Leute

d) Geburt + Tag + Karte

Bilden Sie nun Wortketten aus zusammengesetzten Wörtern mit Ihrem Partner/ Ihrer Partnerin. Nehmen Sie folgende Wörter als Ansatzpunkt:

Mitternacht; Großstadt; Kinderspiel; Parkhaus.

Zum Beispiel: Mitternacht – Nachtarbeit – Arbeitstag – Tag . . .

Vergessen Sie nicht, die neuen Wörter ins Vokabelheft zu schreiben!

KULTUR

LITERATUR

der Absatz (⸚ e)	*paragraph*
die Anschauung (en)	*view*
der/die Antiheld/in (en/nen)	
	antihero/heroine
ausführlich	*detailed*
die Ausgabe (n)	*edition*
der Auszug (⸚ e)	*excerpt*
die Autobiografie (n)	*autobiography*
der/die Autor/in (en/nen)	*author*
der Band (⸚ e)	*volume*
die Belletristik	*fiction and poetry*
der Bestseller (-)	*bestseller*
betonen	*to stress*
der Charakter (e)	*character*
darstellen	*to portray*
der Dialog (e)	*dialogue*
der/die Dichter/in (-/nen)	*poet*
das Drama (-men)	*drama*

die Einleitung (en)	*introduction*
die Epik	*epic*
der/die Erzähler/in (-/nen)	*narrator*
die Erzählung (en)	*narrative*
die Figur (en)	*character*
die Gattung (en)	*genre*
das Gedicht (e)	*poem*
das Gleichnis (se)	*simile*
das Happyend	*happy ending*
die Ironie	*irony*
das Kapitel (-)	*chapter*
der Kassenschlager (-)	*blockbuster*
konkrete Dichtung	*concrete poetry*
der/die Kritiker/in (-/nen)	*critic*
das Leitmotiv (e)	*leitmotif*
die Lyrik	*poetry*
das Meisterwerk (e)	*masterpiece*
die Metapher (n)	*metaphor*
moralisch	*moral*

das jüngste Werk	*the latest work*
in einem lebendigen Stil geschrieben	*written in a lively style*
Arbeiten aus den 30er bis 60er Jahren	*works from the thirties to the sixties*
der europaweit bekannte Schriftsteller	*the author known throughout Europe*
mit Ironie erzählt	*narrated with irony*
das 2000 erschienene Buch	*the book published in 2000*

die Novelle (n)	*novella*
der Roman (e)	*novel*
der/die Philosoph/in (en/nen)	
	philosopher
die Poesie	*poetry*
poetisch	*poetic*
die Prosa	*prose*
die Prosaliteratur	*fiction*
der Realismus	*realism*
die Redensart (en)	*cliché, idiom*
der Reim (e)	*rhyme*
sich reimen (auf)	*to rhyme (with)*
das Sachbuch (⸚ er)	*non-fiction*
die Sage (n)	*legend*
satirisch	*satirical*
der/die Schriftsteller/in (-/nen)	
	author, writer
die Strophe (n)	*verse*
symbolisch	*symbolic*
das Taschenbuch (⸚ er)	*paperback*
die Übersetzung (en)	*translation*
ungekürzt	*unabridged*
vergleichen	*to compare*

veröffentlichen	*to publish*
das Vorwort (e)	*preface*
die Zeile (n)	*line*
zeitgenössisch	*contemporary*
das Zitat (e)	*quote*
zitieren	*to quote*

THEATER

abbilden	*to portray*
aufführen	*to put on*
die Aufführung (en)	*performance*
die (Auf)lösung (en)	*denouement*
auftreten	*to appear*
der Auftritt (e)	*appearance*
ausdrücken	*to express*
ausverkauft	*sold out*
der Beifall (⸚ e)	*applause*
die Besetzung (en)	*cast*
die Bühne (n)	*stage*
die Bühnenausstattung	*props*
das Bühnenbild (er)	*stage set*
die Darstellung (en)	*acting*
der/die Dramatiker/in (-/nen)	*dramatist*

das Buch steht seit 10 Wochen auf der Bestsellerliste	*the book has been on the bestseller list for 10 weeks*
in deutscher Sprache	*in German*
die Zentralfigur dieser Erzählung	*the central character of this story*
sich hineinversetzen in die Lage von X	*to empathise with X's situation*
den Nobelpreis für Literatur erhalten	*to win the Nobel Prize for Literature*

dramaturgisch	*dramatic*	das Programmheft (e)	*programme*
die Generalprobe (n)	*dress rehearsal*	der/die Protagonist/in (en/nen)	
die Gestalt (en)	*figure*		*protagonist*
die Handlung (en)	*plot*	das Publikum	*audience*
die Hauptfigur (en)	*principal character*	der/die Schauspieler/in (-/nen)	*actor*
das Hauptthema (-men)	*main theme*	das Schicksal (e)	*fate*
der Höhepunkt (e)	*highlight*	das Stück (e)	*play*
inszenieren	*to produce*	die Spielleitung (en)	*direction*
die Inszenierung (en)	*production*	die Stimmung (en)	*atmosphere*
das Kabarett (e)	*cabaret*	das Szenenwechsel (-)	*scene change*
die Kulissen (pl)	*scenery, stage set*	das Thema (-men)	*theme*
das Lampenfieber	*stagefright*	die Tragödie (n)	*tragedy*
leiten	*to direct*	die Uraufführung (en)	*premiere*
die Pause (n)	*interval*	vermitteln	*to convey*
die Premiere (n)	*first night*	die Vorschau (en)	*preview*
die Probe (n)	*rehearsal*	die Vorstellung (en)	*performance*

der erste Akt	*first act*
hinter den Kulissen	*backstage*
auf der Bühne sein	*to be on stage*
ein volles Haus	*full house*
sie hat die Isolde dargestellt	*she played the part of Isolde*
X wird immer auf die Bühne gebracht	*X is always being staged*
auf Tournee gehen	*to go on tour*
es wurde mit einem Preis ausgezeichnet	*it won a prize*
eine erfolgreiche Produktion	*a successful production*
das Stück handelt von . . .	*the play is about . . .*
die Szene spielt in Spanien	*the scene takes place in Spain*
es spielt im 16. Jahrhundert	*it takes place in the 16th century*
tosender Beifall	*thunderous applause*

FILM

die Aufnahme (n)	*shot*
die Co-Produktion (en)	*co-production*
das Drehbuch (⁻⁻ er)	*script*
drehen	*to shoot*
der Drehort (e)	*location*
der/die Filmemacher/in (-/nen)	
	film-maker
die Filmmusik (en)	*film music*
der Filmstar (s)	*film star*
die Folge (n)	*sequel*
die Freigabe (n)	*certificate*
die Hauptrolle (n)	*leading role*
der/die Held/in (en/nen)	*hero/heroine*
herausbringen	*to release*
das Kino (s)	*cinema*
der/die Kinogänger/in (-/nen)	
	cinemagoer
der Kinorenner (-)	*box office hit*

laufen	*to run*
die Leinwand (⁻⁻ e)	*screen*
die Nahaufnahme (n)	*close-up*
die Nebenrolle (n)	*supporting role*
präsentieren	*to present*
der/die Produzent/in (en/nen)	*producer*
die Regie	*direction*
Regie führen	*to direct*
der/die Regisseur/in (e/nen)	*director*
die Rolle (n)	*role*
der Szenenaufbau (ten)	*set*
synchronisieren	*to dub*
die Toneffekte (pl)	*sound effects*
die Tricks (pl)	*special effects*
die Verfilmung (en)	*filming*
das Video	*video*
die Vorschau (en)	*trailer*
der Vor-/Nachspann	*credits*
in Zeitlupe	*in slow motion*

eine Rolle spielen	*to play a role*
er hat in diesem Film mitgespielt	*he was in this film*
der Film hat deutsche Untertitel	*the film has German subtitles*
der Film läuft in aller Welt	*the film is showing all over the world*
ein Film in vier Fortsetzungen	*a film in four parts*
bei Außenaufnahmen sein	*to be on location*
sich einen Film ansehen	*to watch a film*
nach dem gleichnamigen Roman von X	*based on the novel of the same name by X*
von Oscar-Preisträger/in X	*by the Oscar winning X*
demnächst in diesem Kino	*coming soon to this cinema*

TANZ

arrangieren	*to arrange*
die Ballerina (-nen)	*ballerina*
das Ballett (e)	*ballet*
die Bewegung (en)	*movement*
der/die Choreograf/in (en/nen)	
	choreographer
die Choreografie	*choreography*
darbieten	*to perform*
das Engagement (s)	*engagement*
der Jazztanz (¨ e)	*jazz dance*
steppen	*to tap dance*
der/die Tänzer/in (-/nen)	*dancer*
die Truppe (n)	*company*

KUNST

abstrakt	*abstract*
das Aquarell (e)	*watercolour*
der Aspekt (e)	*aspect*
das Atelier (s)	*studio*
ausdrucksfähig	*expressive*
die Ausstellung (en)	*exhibition*

der/die Bildhauer/in (-/nen)	*sculptor*
das Design (s)	*design*
die Fotografie	*photography*
die Galerie (n)	*gallery*
der Gegenstand (¨ e)	*object*
die Grafik	*graphic arts*
der Hintergrund (¨ e)	*background*
der Kunstdruck (e)	*art print*
der/die Künstler/in (-/nen)	*artist*
das Kunstmuseum	*art museum*
das Kunstwerk (e)	*work of art*
die Landschaft (en)	*landscape*
moderne Kunst	*modern art*
die Nachahmung (en)	*imitation*
das Oeuvre	*oeuvre*
das Ölgemälde (-)	*oil painting*
das Originalgemälde (-)	
	original painting
die Plastik (en)	*sculpture*
das Porträt (s)	*portrait*
postmodern	*post-modern*
die Radierung (en)	*etching*

tänzerische Darbietung	*dance act*
Ballettstunden nehmen	*to take ballet lessons*
eine Ausbildung in zeitgenössischem Tanz	*training in contemporary dance*
ein vielversprechendes Talent	*a promising talent*
es drückt etwas sehr Wichtiges aus	*it expresses something very important*
moderner Tanz/moderne Kunst	*modern dance/art*
die bildenden Künste	*fine arts*

die Retrospektive (n)	*retrospective*
die Sammlung (en)	*collection*
verewigen	*to immortalise*
der Vordergrund (⸚ e)	*forefront*
die Zeichnung (en)	*drawing*

MUSIK

der Auftakt	*upbeat*
die Blechbläser (pl)	*brass instruments*
der Brit-Pop	*Brit-pop*
die Charts/die Hitliste	*charts*
der Chor (⸚ e)	*choir*
der/die Dirigent/in (en/nen)	*conductor*
einstudieren	*to rehearse*
der Gesang (⸚ e)	*singing*
die Harmonie (n)	*harmony*
die Hitparade (n)	*charts*
die Holzbläser (pl)	*woodwind*
improvisieren	*to improvise*
die Independent-Szene	*independent scene*

das Instrument (e)	*instrument*
instrumental	*instrumental*
der Klang (⸚ e)	*sound*
der/die Komponist/in (en/nen)	*composer*
die Komposition (en)	*composition*
der Konzertsaal (-säle)	*concert hall*
der/die Leadsänger/in (-/nen)	*lead singer*
das Lied (er)	*song*
die Lyrics	*lyrics*
die Melodie (n)	*melody*
melodisch	*melodic*
das Mischpult (e)	*sound mixer*
der/die Musiker/in (-/nen)	*musician*
die Musikindustrie	*music industry*
die Musikszene	*music scene*
die Oper (n)	*opera*
das Orchester (-)	*orchestra*
die Ovation (en)	*ovation*
der Popstar (s)	*pop star*

X ist diese Woche in der Hitparade	*X is in the charts this week*
X ist auf Nummer eins	*X is number one*
ein neues Album herausbringen	*to release a new album*
regelmäßig üben	*to practise regularly*
vom Blatt spielen/Noten lesen	*to sightread/to read music*
klassische/zeitgenössische Musik	*classical/contemporary music*
in vier Sätzen	*in four movements*
absolutes Gehör/nach Gehör spielen	*perfect pitch/to play by ear*
komponiert von	*composed by*

die Probe (n)	*rehearsal*	beklemmend	*oppressive*
der Rhythmus (-men)	*rhythm*	charmant	*charming*
die Rockband (s)	*rock band*	durchschnittlich	*average*
der/die Sänger/in (-/nen)	*singer*	ehrgeizig	*ambitious*
der Schlager (-)	*pop hit*	eindrucksvoll	*impressive*
das Schlagzeug	*percussion*	einmalig	*unique*
die Single (s)	*single*	emotional	*emotional*
der/die Solist/in (en/nen)	*soloist*	enttäuschend	*disappointing*
der Sound	*sound*	experimentell	*experimental*
der Soundtrack (s)	*soundtrack*	erfolgreich	*successful*
die Streicher (pl)	*stringed instruments*	ergreifend	*moving*
die Symphonie/Sinfonie (n)	*symphony*	ernsthaft	*serious*
der Track (s)	*track*	fesselnd	*engrossing*
der Virtuose (n)	*virtuoso (m)*	genießbar	*enjoyable*
die Virtuosin (nen)	*virtuoso (f)*	gewagt	*risqué*
die Vocals	*vocals*	glanzvoll	*brilliant*
der Vortrag (⸚ e)	*recital*	großartig	*splendid*
		handlungsarm	*thin on plot*

KRITIK ÜBEN

		hervorragend	*magnificent*
aktionsreich	*action-packed*	historisch	*historic*
amüsant	*amusing*	innovativ	*innovative*
atemberaubend	*breathtaking*	katastrophal	*disastrous*
ausdrucksintensiv	*expressive*	kompliziert	*complicated*
ausdruckslos	*inexpressive*	kurzweilig	*entertaining*
beachtlich	*remarkable*	lobenswert	*praiseworthy*

X riss den Abend heraus	*X saved the evening*
gute Kritiken bekommen	*to get good reviews*
X gab eine einmalige Vorstellung	*X gave a once in a lifetime performance*
das Schauspiel hat mich mitgerissen	*I was carried along by the play*
ein heiterer/langweiliger Abend	*a merry/boring evening*
nullachtfünfzehn (inf)	*run-of-the-mill*

mittelmäßig	*mediocre*		subjektiv	*subjective*
neuartig	*new*		tiefsinning	*deep*
oberflächlich	*superficial, shallow*		überzeugend	*convincing*
packend	*exciting*		ungewöhnlich	*unusual*
rührselig	*tear-jerking*		unterhaltsam	*entertaining*
sachlich	*objective*		vielversprechend	*promising*
schonungslos	*savage*		virtuos	*virtuoso*
sentimental	*sentimental*		wirkungsvoll	*effective*
stimmungsvoll	*atmospheric*		zeitlos	*timeless*

VOKABELTIPP

Wortspiele (1)

Wenn Sie eine neue Gruppe von Wörtern lernen (zum Beispiel Wörter zum Thema Literatur), können Sie selber damit Wortspiele erfinden.

a) Anagramme – bringen Sie die Buchstaben in die falsche Reihenfolge. Sehen Sie sich die Wörter am nächsten Tag wieder an. Wie viele kennen Sie noch?

U S L M E R A I S

b) Kreuzworträtsel – stellen Sie Fragen und machen Sie ein Kreuzworträtsel. Kann Ihr/e Partner/in das Rätsel lösen?

 (ein kurzer Roman)

¹N | O | V | E | L | L | E | ■

c) Wortsalat – machen Sie einen Wortsalat aus den Wörtern. Kann Ihr/e Partner/in die Wörter finden?

B	O	A	U	T	O	R	I	N	B	V
E	O	V	E	L	L	V	A	G	A	E
L	S	S	S	L	B	U	C	H	T	R
L	O	Q	A	L	L	A	U	R	E	L

45

MEDIEN

FERNSEHEN

aufnehmen	*to record, video*
ausstrahlen	*to broadcast*
die Bildqualität (en)	*picture quality*
das Breitbandfernsehen	*widescreen TV*
einschalten	*to switch on*
die Einschaltquote (n)	*viewing figure*
der Empfang	*reception*
empfangen	*to receive*
das Feature (s)	*feature*
der Fernsehsender (-)	*broadcaster*
die Folge (n)	*episode*
das Frühstücksfernsehen	*breakfast television*
der Glotzkasten (¨) (inf)	*goggle-box*
interaktives Fernsehen	*interactive TV*

das Kabelfernsehen	*cable television*
der/die Kabelteilnehmer/in (-/nen)	*cable viewer*
das Kamerateam (s)	*camera crew*
der Kanal (¨ e)	*channel*
das Kanalhüpfen	*channel-hopping*
die Haupteinschaltzeit (en)	*peak viewing time*
die Lizenzgebühr (en)	*licence fee*
lokal	*local*
die Live-Übertragung (en)	*live broadcast*
die Massenmedien (pl)	*mass media*
das Medienangebot (e)	*choice of media*
das Nachrichtennetzwerk	*news network*

digitales Fernsehen	*digital TV*
das ZDF strahlt den 45-minütigen Film X aus	*ZDF broadcasts the 45-minute film X*
mit Untertiteln für Hörgeschädigte	*with subtitles for the hard of hearing*
regelmäßige Sendungen	*regular programmes*
direkt ins Wohnzimmer gebracht	*beamed straight into the living-room*
die Ziehung der Lottozahlen	*drawing of the lotto numbers*
vor der Glotze hocken (inf)	*to sit in front of the box*
auf Video aufnehmen	*to record on video*
auf Video/DVD ausleihen	*to rent on video/DVD*

das Online-Shopping	*TV shopping*
das Pay-TV	*pay per view TV*
der Programmhinweis (e)	*programme tip*
das Reality-Fernsehen	*reality TV*
per Satellit	*via satellite*
das Satellitenfernsehen	*satellite television*
die Satellitenschüssel (n)	*satellite dish*
die Satellitentechnologie	*satellite technology*
das Schulfernsehen	*school television*
die Sendezeit (en)	*broadcast time*
die Serie (n)	*series*
die Störung (en)	*disturbance*
das Streiflicht (er)	*highlight*
der Teletext	*teletext*
übertragen	*to transmit*
die Unterbrechung (en)	*interruption*
der/die Veranstalter/in (-/nen)	*promoter*
die Vernetzung (en)	*network*
der Videomarkt (¨ e)	*video market*

| die Wiederholung (en) | *repeat* |
| die Zielgruppe (n) | *target audience* |

HÖRFUNK

der Diskjockey (s)	*disc jockey*
die Frequenz (en)	*frequence*
die Funkstation (en)	*radio station*
der/die Hörer/in (-/nen)	*listener*
die Hörfunksendung (en)	*radio show*
das Hörspiel (e)	*radio play*
der/die Interviewer/in (-/nen)	*interviewer*
der/die Moderator/in (en/nen)	*presenter*
der Musiksender (-)	*music station*
das Radio (s)	*radio*
der Radiosender (-)	*radio station*
der/die Rundfunksprecher/in (-/nen)	*radio broadcaster*
die Tonqualität (en)	*sound quality*
die Verkehrsmeldung (en)	*traffic report*
das Wellenband (¨ er)	*waveband*
die Wellenlänge (n)	*wavelength*

digitales Radio	*digital radio*
auf ein anderes Programm umschalten	*to switch over to another channel*
am Mikrofon: Matthias Holtmann	*the presenter is Matthias Holtmann*
Radio Bremen einschalten	*to tune into Radio Bremen*
regionales Programm	*regional programme*
live im Studio	*live from the studio*
es wird in stereo übertragen	*broadcast in stereo*

PRESSE

das Abonnement (s)	*subscription*
der/die Abonnent/in (en/nen)	
	subscriber
der Artikel (-)	*article*
aufhetzen	*to incite*
der Beitrag (÷ e)	*contribution*
der Bericht (e)	*report*
die Boulevardpresse	*gutter press*
die Dokumentation (en)	*documentation*
drucken	*to print*
die Fachzeitschrift (en)	*trade magazine*
das Feuilleton (s)	*feature pages*
illustriert	*illustrated*
die Illustrierte (n)	*magazine*
der Herausgeber (-)	*publisher*
der Hintergrundbericht (e)	
	background report
die Informationsfreiheit (en)	
	freedom of information
die Informationsvielfalt	
	diversity of information

informieren	*to inform*
der Journalismus	*journalism*
die Klatschspalte (n)	*gossip column*
der Kommentar (e)	*commentary*
der/die Korrespondent/in (en/nen)	
	correspondent
der Leitartikel (-)	*editorial*
der Leserkreis (e)	*readership*
die Meldung (en)	*announcement*
monatlich	*monthly*
die Nachricht (en)	*news item*
die Pressefreiheit	*freedom of the press*
die Presseinformation (en)	
	press release
die Pressekonferenz (en)	
	press conference
die Recherche (n)	*investigation*
der/die Redakteur/in (e/nen)	*editor*
die Redaktion (en)	*editorial office*
die Regenbogenpresse	*gutter press*
die Reportage (n)	*report*
der/die Reporter/in (-/nen)	*reporter*

eine angesehene Zeitung	*a quality newspaper*
eine Zeitung abonnieren	*to subscribe to a newspaper*
Schlagzeilen machen	*to make the headlines*
wöchentliche/tägliche Erscheinungsweise	*appearing weekly/daily*
objektive Berichterstattung	*objective reporting*
die öffentliche Aufgabe der Presse	*the public duty of the press*
käuflicher Journalismus	*chequebook journalism*
etwas an die Presse durchsickern lassen	*to leak something to the newspapers*
einer Zeitung Exklusivrechte geben	*to give exclusive rights to a newspaper*

die Schlagzeile (n)	*headline*
selbstregulierend	*self-regulating*
die Spalte (n)	*column*
der Sportteil (e)	*sports section*
die Tageszeitung (en)	*daily paper*
das Urheberrecht (e)	*copyright*
die Verbreitung (en)	*dissemination*
verleumderisch	*libellous*
die Verleumdung (en)	*libel*
die Wochenzeitung (en)	*weekly paper*
der Zeitungsausschnitt (e)	*clipping*

WERBUNG

das Anzeigenblatt (± er)	*advertiser (paper)*
beeinflussen	*to influence*
die Kleinanzeige (n)	*classified advert*

die Marke (n)	*brand*
die Markenware	*branded goods*
das Plakat (e)	*poster*
die Reklame (n)	*advert*
die Reklametafel (n)	*billboard*
die Schleichwerbung (en)	*plug*
der Slogan (s)	*slogan*
überreden	*to persuade*
überzeugen	*to convince*
der/die Verbraucher/in (-/nen)	*consumer*
die Verkaufskampagne (n)	*sales campaign*
die Werbeagentur (en)	*advertising agency*
der Werbespot (s)	*commercial break*
der Werbespruch (± e)	*jingle*

die Welt der Jugendlichen ist von . . . geprägt	*young people's lives are influenced by . . .*
X ist von der Werbung abhängig	*X is dependent on advertising*
das beeinflusst das Leben von Millionen Menschen	*it influences the lives of millions*
jemandem einreden, dass . . .	*to brainwash someone into thinking that . . .*
einen Einfluss ausüben	*to have an effect*

Definitionen

Wenn Sie neue Wörter lernen, brauchen Sie nicht immer eine englische Bedeutung dafür. Manchmal hilft es Ihnen mehr, wenn Sie eine Definition davon machen oder andere deutsche Wörter dafür finden.

die Korrespondentin – eine Frau, die für die Medien berichtet

Schreiben Sie für die folgenden Wörter deutsche Definitionen auf.

die Pressekonferenz

übertragen

die Kurzmeldung

die Zielgruppe

die Funkstation

die Informationsvielfalt

vermitteln

die Boulevardpresse

Wenn Sie jetzt neue Wörter lernen, denken Sie sich eine Definition aus.

MENSCHEN

JUGENDLICHE

sich entwickeln	*to develop*
erreichen	*to achieve*
sich finden	*to find yourself*
die Klubszene	*club scene*
die Klubkultur	*club culture*
der Generationsunterschied (e)	*generation gap*
jugendgefährdend	*harmful to young people*
die Jugendkriminalität	*juvenile delinquency*
jugendlicher Straftäter	*juvenile delinquent*
die Jugendkultur	*teenage culture*

das Piercing (s)	*piercing*
rebellieren	*to rebel*
die Straßenbande (n)	*street gang*
die Unabhängigkeit	*independence*
die Unterstützung	*support*
verletzbar	*vulnerable*
verantwortlich	*responsible*

RECHTE UND PFLICHTEN

der/die Bürger/in (-/nen)	*citizen*
die Folgerung/Auswirkung (en)	*implication*
der Führerschein (e)	*driving licence*
hilfreich	*willing to help*

das Recht haben, etwas zu tun	*to be entitled to do something*
in Pflege sein	*to be in care*
alt genug sein, um etwas zu tun	*to be old enough to do something*
jemanden auf seine Verantwortung aufmerksam machen	*to make somebody aware of their responsibilities*
ein Bewusstsein für gesellschaftliche Verantwortung haben	*to have a sense of civic responsibilities*
für sich selber sorgen	*to take care of yourself*
in die Klubs gehen	*to go clubbing*
auf einen Rave gehen	*to go to a rave*
von zu Hause ausziehen	*to leave home*
aufwachsen/erwachsen werden	*to grow up*

ichbezogen/egoistisch	*self-centred*
kindisch	*childish*
minderjährig	*under 18*
die Moral	*morality*
die Pflicht (en)	*duty*
das Plichtbewusstsein	*sense of duty*
die Rechte (pl)	*rights*
reif	*mature*
die Reife	*maturity*
reifen	*to mature*
die Verantwortung	*responsibility*
volljährig	*over 18*
das Wahlrecht	*the right to vote*
der Wehrdienst	
	national service (military)
der Zivildienst	
	national service (community)

FAMILIE

das Adoptivkind (er)	*adopted child*

das Aupairmädchen	*au-pair*
entführt werden	*to be abducted*
die Familiengesetze	
	family-friendly policies
die Familienwerte (pl)	*family values*
der/die Fürsorgeberechtigte	*guardian*
die Kindererziehung	
	upbringing of children
das Kindergeld	*child benefit*
Kinder großziehen	*to raise a family*
das Kindermädchen	*nanny*
die Kindertagesstätte (n)	*creche*
die Kindesmisshandlung	*child abuse*
der Nachwuchs	*offspring*
der Paedophile (n)	*paedophile*
das Pflegeheim	*residential care home*
das Pflegekind (er)	*foster child*
das Schlüsselkind (er)	*latchkey child*
die Tagesmutter (¨)	*childminder*
überbehütet	*over-protected*

die Verantwortung übernehmen	*to take responsibility*
erfolgreich sein im Leben	*to succeed in life*
individuelle Freiheit	*personal freedom*
volljährig werden	*to come of age*
elterliche Zustimmung	*parental consent*
verantwortlich vor dem Gesetz	*legally responsible*
für seine Handlungen verantwortlich sein	*to be responsible for your actions*
Handlungen haben Konsequenzen	*actions have consequences*
unverantwortlich handeln	*to act irresponsibly*

PARTNERSCHAFT

alleinstehend sein	*to be single*
die Auseinandersetzung (en)	*argument*
die Beziehung (en)	*relationship*
der Bigamist (en)	*bigamist*
bisexuell	*bisexual*
das Blind Date	*blind date*
die Ehe (n)	*marriage*
der Ehebruch (⁻ e)	*adultery*
das Ehemündigkeitsalter	*age of consent*
die Ehrlichkeit	*honesty*
die Familienplanung	*family planning*
fremdgehen	*to have an affair*
das Gefühl (e)	*feeling*
der/die Geliebte (n)	*lover*

der Geschlechtsverkehr	*sexual intercourse*
die Hausarbeit (en)	*housework*
die Hausfrau (en)	*housewife*
der Hausmann (⁻ er)	*house husband*
heiraten	*to get married*
heterosexuell	*heterosexual*
homosexuell	*homosexual*
der Konflikt (e)	*conflict*
der/die Lebensgefährte/gefährtin (n/nen)	*common-law husband/wife*
lesbisch	*lesbian*
die Liebe	*love*
die Menschlichkeit	*humanity*
die Offenheit	*openness*
das Onlinedating	*online dating*
der/die Partner/in (-/nen)	*partner*

eine Familie gründen	*to start a family*
in einer stabilen Gemeinschaft erzogen werden	*to be brought up in a stable environment*
eine glückliche Kindheit genießen	*to have a happy childhood*
eine benachteiligte Kindheit haben	*to have a deprived childhood*
die enge Familie	*nuclear family*
alleinerziehende/r Mutter/Vater	*single-parent family*
die erweiterte Familie	*extended family*
Konflikte zwischen Eltern und Kindern	*parent-child conflict*
Mangel an Pflegefamilien	*shortage of foster places*
das Besuchsrecht für die Kinder	*right of access to your children*
unter Misshandlung leiden	*to suffer abuse*
die Kinder loslassen	*to let go of your childen*

das Partnervermittlungsbüro (s)	dating agency
der Respekt	respect
sich scheiden lassen	to get divorced
die Scheidung (en)	divorce
die Schwiegereltern (pl)	parents-in-law
sexistisch	sexist
der Single (s)	single person
die Spermabank (en)	sperm bank
die Toleranz	tolerance
die Trennung (en)	separation
die Treue	fidelity
treu sein	to be faithful
die Verhütung	contraception
verlassen	to abandon
sich verlieben	to fall in love
sich verloben	to get engaged
das Verständnis	understanding
das Vorbild (er)	role model
die Zuneigung (en)	affection
zusammenleben	to live together
zusammenziehen	to move in together

FRAUEN

berufsorientiert	career-orientated
die Chancengleichheit	equal opportunities
die Eigenständigkeit	independence
der Eisprung (⸚ e)	ovulation
emanzipiert	liberated
erfolgreich	successful
die Fehlgeburt (e)	miscarriage
der Feminismus	feminism
die Feministin (nen)	feminist
die Frauenbelange (pl)	women's issues
die Frauenbewegung (en)	feminist movement
die Frauenemanzipation	emancipation of women
die Frauengruppe (n)	women's group
das Frauenhaus (⸚ er)	refuge for battered women
die Frauenmisshandlung (en)	wife battering

sich zum Date verabreden	to go on a date
Verhütungsmittel benutzen	to use contraceptives
die Unschuld verlieren	to lose your virginity
Unterstützung vom Partner/von der Partnerin	support from the partner
den Partner/die Partnerin verlassen	to leave your partner
Ehebruch begehen	to commit adultery
die platonische Beziehung	platonic relationship
das Zölibat befolgen	to be celibate

die Frauenrechte (pl)	*women's rights*
die Gleichberechtigung (en)	*equality*
die Kinderbetreuung (en)	*childcare*
die Leihmutter (⸚)	*surrogate mother*
die Mütterlichkeit	*motherliness*
die Mutterschaft	*motherhood*
die Periode (n)	*period*
die Pille nehmen	*to be on the pill*
die Rabenmutter (⸚)	*bad mother*
das Retortenbaby (s)	*test-tube baby*
die Schwangerschaft (en)	*pregnancy*
die Schwangerschaftsvertretung (en)	*maternity cover*
die Selbstbestätigung	*self-affirmation*
sich verwirklichen	*to fulfil yourself*

unfruchtbar	*infertile*
die Wechseljahre (pl)	*menopause*
die Weiblichkeit	*femininity*

ALTER

der/die Altenpfleger/in (-/nen)	*old people's nurse*
die Altentagesstätte (n)	*old people's day centre*
die Altersbeschwerden (pl)	*complaints of old age*
das Altersheim (e)	*old people's home*
die Altersrente (n)	*old age pension*
das Altersruhegeld (er)	*retirement benefit*

Kinder, Küche, Kirche	*children, kitchen and church (women's traditional role)*
die Strohwitwe (n)	*"straw widow": a woman left to look after the children while her husband is away working*
eine unfähige Mutter	*an unfit mother*
im gebärfähigen Alter	*of childbearing age*
der Aufstieg der Frauen in die Chefetagen	*promotion of women to high-powered positions*
zum Beruf zurückkehren	*to return to a career*
sexuelle Belästigung (en)	*sexual harassment*
Hormonbehandlung in den Wechseljahren	*HRT treatment*
für gleichberechtigte Bezahlung kämpfen	*to fight for equal pay*
künstliche Befruchtung	*IVF*
die biologische Uhr	*the biological clock*

die Altersschwäche (n) — *infirmity*

die Altersversorgung (en) — *provision for old age*

das Hospiz (e) — *hospice*

kenntnisreich — *knowledgeable*

die Lebensversicherung (en) — *life insurance*

die Menschenwürde — *human dignity*

pensioniert — *retired*

die Pensionierung (en) — *retirement*

pflegebedürftig — *in need of care*

der Pflegefall (⸚ e) — *a person who requires nursing*

das Pflegeheim (e) — *nursing home*

das Pflegepersonal — *nursing staff*

der/die Rentner/in (-/nen) — *senior citizen, old age pensioner*

der Ruhestand — *retirement*

die Rundumpflege — *round the clock care*

rüstig — *sprightly*

senil — *senile*

die Senilität — *senile dementia*

die Sterbehilfe — *euthanasia*

der/die Verwandte (n) — *relative*

die Verwandtschaft — *relations*

zerbrechlich — *fragile*

---

etwas zur Gesellschaft beitragen — *to contribute to society*

das Ausscheiden aus dem Arbeitsleben — *retirement (stopping work)*

in den Ruhestand treten — *to retire*

in Vorruhestand gehen — *to take early retirement*

sich an den Ruhestand gewöhnen — *to adjust to retirement*

die alternde Generation — *the ageing population*

die Menschen leben länger — *people are living longer*

der/die abhängige Angehörige (n) — *dependent*

die Pflege von alten Menschen — *care of the elderly*

Wohnungen für Senioren — *sheltered housing*

ans Haus gefesselt sein — *to be house-bound*

im Rollstuhl sitzen — *to be in a wheelchair*

Essen auf Rädern — *meals on wheels*

VOKABELTIPP

Wortfamilien

Wenn Sie ein neues Wort lernen, lernen Sie gleichzeitig die Familienmitglieder kennen!

Auf Seite 56 sehen Sie zum Beispiel das Wort *kenntnisreich – knowledgeable.*

Wie heißen folgende Familienmitglieder auf Englisch?

a) die Kenntnis   b) kennen lernen   c) der Kenner   d) kennerisch

Vergessen Sie auch den weiteren Familienkreis nicht!
Wie heißen folgende Wörter auf Englisch?

e) das Kennwort   f) das Kennzeichen   g) die Kennziffer

Wählen Sie vier Wörter, die Sie vor kurzem gelernt haben. Schlagen Sie sie jetzt im Wörterbuch nach. Schreiben Sie so viele Familienmitglieder wie möglich auf.

SCHULE

SCHULTYPEN

die Abendschule (n)	*night school*
der Kindergarten (÷)	*kindergarten*
die Berufsschule (n)	*vocational school*
die Gesamtschule (n)	
	comprehensive school
die Grundschule (n)	*primary school*
das Gymnasium (-ien)	*grammar school*
die Hauptschule (n)	
	secondary school (age 10–15)
das Internat (e)	*boarding school*
die Privatschule (n)	*private school*
die Realschule (n)	
	secondary school (age 10–16)
die Sonderschule (n)	
	special needs school
die staatliche Schule (n)	*state school*

SCHULPRÜFUNGEN

bestehen	*to pass*
beurteilen	*to assess*
durchfallen	*to fail*
die Klassenarbeit (en)	*(written) test*
die Klausur (en)	*exam, paper*
lernen	*to revise*
der Leistungsdruck	
	pressure to achieve good grades
mittlere Reife	*Realschule qualification at end of year 10*
mündlich	*oral*
pauken	*to cram*
die Prüfung (en)	*exam*
die Qualifikation (en)	*qualification*

das Abitur	*grammar school exam at end of year 13 (like A-Level)*
eine schriftliche Prüfung ablegen	*to take a written exam*
gute/schlechte Noten bekommen	*to get good/bad grades*
sehr gut (1)	*very good*
gut (2)	*good*
befriedigend (3)	*satisfactory*
ausreichend (4)	*fair*
mangelhaft (5)	*poor*
ungenügend (6)	*unsatisfactory*

IN DER SCHULE

der/die Abiturient/in (en/nen)

person taking the Abitur exam

die AG (s) (Arbeitsgemeinschaft)

extra-curricular activity group

das Bildungssystem (e)

education system

der Elternabend (e) *parents' evening*

der Elternbeirat (⁓ e)

parents' committee

der/die Elternvertreter/in (-/nen)

parent representative

der/die Lehrer/in (-/nen) *teacher*

das Lehrerkollegium

(body of) teachers, staff

die Lehrerversammlung (en)

staff meeting

der Lehrplan (⁓ e) *syllabus*

der Personalrat (⁓ e) *staff committee*

die Projekttage (pl) *project days*

der/die Referendar/in (e/nen)

student teacher

der Schulbeirat (⁓ e) *school governor*

der/die Schuldirektor/in (en/nen)

headteacher

die Schulferien (pl) *school holidays*

das Schuljahr (e) *school year*

die Schulordnung (en) *school rules*

der/die Schulsprecher/in (-/nen)

head boy/girl

der Stundenplan (⁓ e) *timetable*

der/die Streber/in (-/nen) *swot*

das Trimester (-) *term*

die Vertretung (en) *supply teacher*

das Zeugnis (se) *report*

PROBLEME

abschreiben *to copy, cheat*

mogeln *to cheat*

die Nachhilfe *extra coaching*

das Nachsitzen *detention*

petzen *to tell tales*

die Prügel (pl) *beating*

die Prügelei (en) *fight*

der Randalierer (-) *troublemaker*

der/die Vertrauenslehrer/in (-/nen) *liaison teacher (between pupils and staff)*

die allgemeine Schulpflicht *compulsory school attendance*

in der Schülermitverwaltung (SMV) *on the student committee*

Klassensprecher/in der Klasse 10V sein *to be the class representative of class 10V*

fächerübergreifender Unterricht *cross-curricular lesson*

Samstag ist schulfrei *there's no school on Saturday*

hitzefrei haben *to have the day off because of hot weather*

der Rowdy (s)	*bully*
die Schikane (n)	*bullying*
schlechtes Benehmen	*bad behaviour*
schwänzen	*to skive, play truant*
sitzen bleiben	*to repeat a year*
störend	*disruptive*
zurückschlagen	*to hit back*

NACH DER SCHULZEIT

der/die Absolvent/in (en/nen)	*graduate*
absolvieren	*to complete (a course)*
die Akademie (n)	*academy*
der/die Azubi (s)	*trainee*
das BAföG	*student loan*
die Berufsakademie (n)	*vocationally orientated college*

der Doktortitel (-)	*doctorate*
der/die Dozent/in (en/nen)	*lecturer*
der Fachbereich (e)	*field (of study)*
die Fachhochschule (n)	*technical college*
die Fakultät (en)	*faculty*
die Forschung (en)	*research*
die Fortbildung	*further education*
die Hochschule (n)	*college, university*
die Lehre (n)	*apprenticeship*
die Lehrerausbildung	*teacher training*
der Lehrling (e)	*apprentice*
die Lerngruppe (n)	*study group*
der/die Professor/in (en/nen)	*professor*
promovieren	*to do a PhD*
das Semester (-)	*semester*
das Stipendium (-ien)	*scholarship*
der/die Student/in (en/nen)	*student*

überfüllte Klassen	*overfilled classes*
(auf Dauer) ausgeschlossen sein	*to be (permanently) excluded*
die Schulgesetze brechen	*to break the school rules*
sich weigern, die Schulgesetze zu befolgen	*to refuse to comply with the school rules*
Schüler/innen mit Lernproblemen	*pupils with learning difficulties*
X zeigt auffälliges Verhalten	*X has behavioural problems*
die Lehrer-Schüler-Beziehung	*teacher-pupil relationship*
eine Schule mit einem schlechten Ruf	*a failing school*
schlechte Einrichtungen (pl)	*poor facilities*
Drogen in Schulen	*drugs in schools*
jeder dritte Schüler hat Angst vor Gewalt	*every third pupil is afraid of violence*
bewaffnete Schüler/innen	*pupils carrying weapons*

das Studentenwohnheim (e)
hall of residence

die Studiendauer *duration of studies*

die Studienfinanzierung (en)
financing of studies

die Studiengebühren (pl) *course fees*

der Studienplatz (∺ e)
university place

die Vorlesung (en) *lecture*

die Weiterbildung *further education*

die Zimmervermittlung (en)
accommodation service

eine abgeschlossene Berufsausbildung haben — *to have completed your training*

das Studium abbrechen — *to drop out of your course*

deutsche Studenten machen ihr Examen im Durchschnitt mit 28,5 Jahren — *German students graduate at an average age of 28.5 years*

berufsorientierter Kurs — *vocational course*

einen Lehrauftrag annehmen — *to take up a lectureship*

das Fach ist mit einem Numerus clausus belegt — *this course has restricted entry*

Materialien anfordern

Wenn Sie sich über ein Thema informieren wollen, können Sie selber
Materialien aus Deutschland sammeln. So bekommen Sie (meistens kostenlos)
deutsche Prospekte, Broschüren und Flugblätter, die Ihnen beim Studium viel
helfen können. Unten steht ein Musterbrief, den Sie benutzen können.
Auf den Seiten 95–96 finden Sie auch eine Liste von Internetadressen.
Fordern Sie selber Materialien an!

[Ihre Adresse]

Pressestelle
[Zieladresse]
[Datum]

Sehr geehrte Damen und Herren,

zur Zeit bin ich Schüler(in) in England und brauche für den
Deutschunterricht Materialien zum Thema **Das Deutsche
Schulsystem**. Bitte schicken Sie (kostenlose) Broschüren zu diesem
Thema sowie eine Liste Ihrer Publikationen, falls vorhanden, an die
obengenannte Adresse.

Vielen Dank im Voraus für Ihre Mühe.

Mit freundlichen Grüßen

[Unterschrift]

SOZIALE PROBLEME

ARBEITSLOSIGKEIT

die Abfindung (en)
redundancy payment

die Abgeschnittenheit *isolation*

das Arbeitsamt (– er) *job centre*

der/die Arbeitsberater/in (-/nen)
careers advisor

die Arbeitsberatung (en)
careers advice

arbeitslos *unemployed*

das Arbeitslosengeld (er)
unemployment benefit

der Arbeitsmangel *lack of work*

der Arbeitsmarkt (– e) *job market*

die Arbeitsvermittlung (en)
employment exchange/agency

die Aussichtslosigkeit *hopelessness*

die Depression (en) *depression*

entlassen werden
to be made redundant

die Entlassung (en) *dismissal*

kündigen *to resign*

die Kündigung (en) *notice*

die Langeweile *boredom*

die Massenarbeitslosigkeit
mass unemployment

der Personalabbau *staff cutbacks*

rausfliegen (inf) *to get the sack*

sich arbeitslos melden	*to register unemployed*
der Antrag auf Arbeitslosengeld	*application for unemployment benefit*
Anspruch auf Arbeitslosengeld haben	*to be entitled to unemployment benefit*
auf Sozialhilfe angewiesen sein	*to rely on social security*
einen Arbeitsplatz suchen/verlieren	*to look for/lose a job*
die Arbeitslosenzahlen sind gestiegen/ gefallen	*the unemployment rate has risen/fallen*
Arbeitsplätze schaffen/streichen	*to create/cut jobs*
Arbeitsbeschaffungsmaßnahme (ABM)	*job creation scheme*
Teilzeitjobs statt Massenentlassungen	*part-time jobs instead of mass redundancies*
sich unnütz vorkommen	*to feel useless*
keine Perspektiven haben	*to have no prospects*

die Selbstachtung — *self-esteem*

das Selbstvertrauen — *self-confidence*

der Sozialhilfebetrüger/in (-/in) — *benefit fraudster*

der/die Sozialhilfeempfänger/in (-/nen) — *person on social security*

die Umschulung (en) — *retraining*

die Vollbeschäftigung — *full employment*

OBDACHLOSIGKEIT

die Armut — *poverty*

der Armutskreislauf (⁼ e) — *poverty cycle*

betteln — *to beg*

das Elend — *misery*

die Gesellschaft ablehnen — *to reject society*

der/die Hausbesetzer/in (-/nen) — *squatter*

die Innenstadt (⁼ e) — *inner city*

der Landstreicher (-) — *tramp*

der/die Obdachlose (n) *homeless person*

das Obdachlosenheim (e) — *hostel for the homeless*

die Obdachlosenhilfe — *soup kitchen*

die Obdachlosensiedlung (en) — *housing scheme for the homeless*

der Pappkarton (s) — *cardboard box*

schnorren — *to scrounge*

sozial benachteiligt — *socially deprived*

sozialer Abstieg — *falling on hard times*

Staatsbürger/in zweiter Klasse — *second class citizen*

sozial ausgeschlossen sein	*to be socially excluded*
am Existenzminimum leben	*to live on the subsistence level*
unter der Armutsgrenze leben	*to live below the poverty line*
in der Armutsfalle gefangen sein	*to be caught in the poverty trap*
im Freien schlafen	*to sleep rough*
erbärmliche Verhältnisse	*squalor*
in beengten Verhältnissen wohnen	*to live in cramped conditions*
unhygienische Wohnverhältnisse	*insanitary living conditions*
ohne festen Wohnsitz	*of no fixed abode*
von Ort zu Ort ziehen	*to wander from place to place*
von zu Hause weglaufen	*to run away from home*
zur Räumung gezwungen werden	*to be evicted*
zu Hause rausgeschmissen werden	*to be thrown out of your home*
das Haus wieder in Besitz nehmen	*to repossess a house*

der/die Straßenmusikant/in (en/nen)

busker

überleben — *to survive*

unterbringen — *to (re)house*

der/die Vermisste (n) — *missing person*

die Wohlstandsgesellschaft

affluent society

das Wohngeld (er) — *housing benefit*

die Wohnungsnot (– e)

housing shortage

der Wohnungsverlust (e) — *loss of home*

VERBRECHEN

der/die Angreifer/in (-/nen) — *attacker*

der/die Autodieb/in (e/nen) — *car thief*

bedrohen — *to threaten*

der Betrug — *fraud*

bewaffnet — *armed*

der Bombenanschlag (– e) — *bomb attack*

die Brandstiftung (en) — *arson*

der/die Dieb/in (e/nen) — *thief*

der Einbruch (– e) — *burglary*

entführen — *to kidnap*

die Erpressung (en) — *blackmail*

gravierend — *serious*

die Handwaffe (n) — *handgun*

illegal — *illegal*

die Körperverletzung (en) — *assault*

kriminell — *criminal*

der Ladendiebstahl (– e) — *shop lifting*

die Messerstecherei (en) — *knifing*

der/die Mörder/in (-/nen) — *murderer*

die Nulltoleranz — *zero tolerance*

das Opfer (-) — *victim*

organisiertes Verbrechen

organised crime

der Raubüberfall (– e) — *robbery*

die Razzia (-ien) — *raid*

der Schaufenstereinbruch (– e)

smash-and-grab raid

eine Straftat begehen

to commit a crime

die Straßenkriminalität — *street crime*

der Straßenraub — *mugging*

unter Beobachtung sein	*to be under surveillance*
großen Schaden anrichten	*to do a lot of damage*
der Unfall mit Fahrerflucht	*hit-and-run accident*
einfacher Diebstahl	*petty theft*
eine organisierte Bande	*an organised gang*
die Bekämpfung der Kriminalität	*the fight against crime*
jemanden gegen seinen Willen beobachten und verfolgen	*to stalk somebody*

65

der Terrorismus	*terrorism*
der Totschlag	*manslaughter*
der/die Übeltäter/in (-/nen)	*wrongdoer*
überfallen	*to attack*
der Vandalismus	*vandalism*
die Verbrechensrate (n)	*crime rate*
die Verbrechensverhütung	*crime prevention*
die Verbrechenswelle (n)	*crime wave*
die Vergewaltigung (en)	*rape*
der Verkehrsrowdy	*road rage (person)*
zusammenschlagen	*to beat up*

GERICHT

angeblich	*alleged*
der/die Angeklagte (n)	*defendant*
anklagen	*to accuse*
Berufung einlegen	*to appeal*
einen Eid ablegen	*to take an oath*
das Fehlurteil (e)	*miscarriage of justice*

die Freiheitsstrafe (n)	*prison sentence*
die Gegenüberstellung (en)	*identity parade*
die Geldstrafe (n)	*fine*
das Gerichtsverfahren (-)	*trial*
das Indiz (ien)	*piece of evidence*
inhaftieren	*to take into custody*
die Justiz	*judiciary (institution)*
das Kreuzverhör (e)	*cross-examination*
der Meineid	*perjury*
der Rechtsanwalt (¨ e)	*lawyer, barrister (m)*
die Rechtsanwältin (nen)	*lawyer, barrister (f)*
die Rechtsverletzung (en)	*breach of the law*
der/die Richter/in (-/nen)	*judge*
die Schöffen (pl)	*jury*
schuldig	*guilty*
der Sozialdienst (e)	*community service*

gegen Kaution freigelassen werden	*to be let out on bail*
wiederholt straffällig sein	*to re-offend*
vor Gericht erscheinen	*to appear before court*
jemanden verklagen	*to take someone to court*
einen Prozess gewinnen/verlieren	*to win/lose a case*
der mutmaßliche Täter	*the presumed culprit*
jemanden in Verdacht haben	*to suspect someone*
angeklagt wegen dreifachen Mordes	*charged for three murders*
jemandem eine Sache anhängen	*to frame someone*

das Strafgericht (e)	*criminal court*
strafrechtlich verfolgen	*to prosecute*
das Strafverfahren	
	criminal proceedings
die Todesstrafe (n)	*death penalty*
der Verdacht	*suspicion*
verhaften	*to arrest*
verklagen	*to sue*
verteidigen	*to defend*
verurteilen	*to convict*
der Zeuge (n)	*witness (m)*
die Zeugin (nen)	*witness (f)*

GEFÄNGNIS

die Bewährung	*probation*
der/die Einsitzende (n)	*inmate*
einsperren	*to lock up*
der/die Erstinhaftierte (n)	
	prisoner for the first time
die Festnahme (n)	*arrest*

das Frauengefängnis (se)	
	women's prison
freilassen	*to release, set free*
der Haftbefehl (e)	*warrant*
der Häftling (e)	*prisoner*
die Haftstrafe (n)	*prison sentence*
die Jugendstrafanstalt (en)	
	young offenders centre
der Knast (inf)	*jail*
die Platznot	*lack of space*
die Resozialisierung (en)	*rehabilitation*
die Sicherungshaft	
	isolation for security reasons
der/die Strafgefangene (n)	*detainee*
der Strafvollzug	*penal system*
überfüllt	*overcrowded*
vorbestraft	*previously convicted*
der/die Wärter/in (-/nen)	*warder*
die Wiedereingliederung	
	reintegration
die Zelle (n)	*cell*

überfüllte Gefängnisse	*overcrowded jails*
zu zwei Jahren verurteilt	*sentenced to two years' imprisonment*
lebenslänglich bekommen	*to serve a life sentence*
Selbstmord begehen	*to commit suicide*
unschuldig verurteilt werden	*to be wrongly convicted*

VOKABELTIPP

Wortspiele (2)

Wenn Sie eine neue Gruppe von Wörtern lernen (zum Beispiel Wörter
zum Thema Obdachlosigkeit), können Sie selber damit Wortspiele erfinden.

a) Wortsteine – wählen Sie ein langes Wort und bilden Sie dann kleinere
Wörter aus den Buchstaben.

    WOHLSTANDSGESELLSCHAFT – (*wohl, stehen, Schaf, Wand, . . .*)

b) Wortassoziation – wählen Sie ein Wort. Dann schreiben Sie andere
Wörter auf, die mit diesem Wort eine Verbindung haben.

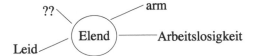

DIE UMWELT

ALLGEMEINES

die Emissionen (pl)   *emissions*

die Erosion   *erosion*

das FCKW-freie Produkt (e)
CFC-free product

gesundheitsgefährdend
dangerous for your health

ökologisch   *ecological*

das Öko-Image   *ecological image*

das Ökosystem (e)   *ecological system*

die Ölverschmutzung (en)   *oil spill*

das Ozonloch (⸚ er)
hole in the ozone layer

die Ozonschicht (en)   *ozone layer*

die Ozonwerte (pl)   *ozone levels*

die Ozonzerstörung
destruction of the ozone layer

der Treibhauseffekt (e)
greenhouse effect

die Treibhausgase (pl)
greenhouse gases

die Umweltbelastung (en)
burden to the environment

umweltbewusst leben
to lead a green lifestyle

umweltfreundlich
environmentally friendly

die Umweltkatastrophe (n)
environmental disaster

umweltschädlich
harmful to the environment

der Umweltschutz
environmental protection

die Umweltverschmutzung
environmental pollution

der Müslimensch (en)	*a person leading an extremely green and wholesome lifestyle*
die globale Verantwortung	*global responsibility*
etwas dagegen unternehmen	*to do something against it*
sich für die Umwelt einsetzen	*to campaign for the environment*
Mitglied einer Aktionsgruppe sein	*to be a member of an action group*
an einer Initiative teilnehmen	*to take part in an initiative*
der/die umweltbewusste Verbraucher/in (-/nen)	*environmentally aware consumer*
Veränderungen im Ökosystem	*changes in the ecosystem*

die Vermeidung	*avoidance*
die Verminderung	*reduction*
die Verschmutzung	*pollution*
die Wasserverschmutzung	
	water pollution

URSACHEN

das Abgas (e)	*exhaust fumes, waste gas*
die Auspuffgase (pl)	*exhaust fumes*
das Chlor	*chlorine*
der Dünger (-)	*fertiliser*
das FCKW	*CFC*
der Giftmüll	*toxic waste*
die Klimaanlage (n)	*air conditioner*
das Kohlendioxid	*carbon dioxide*
das Methan	*methane*
das Pestizid (e)	*pesticide*
das Phosphat	*phosphate*

das Quecksilber	*mercury*
der Sauerstoff	*oxygen*
der Schadstoff (e)	*pollutant*
das Schwefel- und Stickstoffoxid	
	sulphur and nitrogen oxide
das Schwermetall (e)	*heavy metal*
die Spraydose (n)	*aerosol*
die Stickoxid-Emissionen (pl)	
	nitrogen emissions
das Styropor	*polystyrene*
das Treibgas (e)	*propellant*

ENERGIE

der Atommüll	*radioactive waste*
der Atomreaktor	*nuclear reactor*
die Biomasse	*biomass*
der Energieverbrauch	
	energy consumption

der saure Regen	*acid rain*
der Abbau der Ozonschicht	*depletion of the ozone layer*
die schützende Ozonschicht	*the protective ozone layer*
die ozonschädigenden Substanzen	*substances which harm the ozone layer*
die ultraviolette (UV-) Strahlung	*ultraviolet (UV) radiation*
das verbleite Benzin	*leaded petrol*
nicht erneuerbare Energie	*finite energy*
die erneuerbaren Energien (pl)	*renewable energy sources*
durch Wasserkraft erzeugte Energie	*hydro-electric power*
die fossilen Energieträger (pl)	*fossil fuels*
alternative Energiequellen suchen	*to look for alternative sources of energy*

das Erdöl	*oil*
das Gas	*natural gas*
die Geothermie	*geothermal power*
die Kernenergie	*nuclear energy*
das Kernkraftwerk (e)	
	nuclear power station
die Kohle	*coal*
das Kraftwerk (e)	*power station*
die Solarenergie	*solar energy*
solarbetrieben	*solar-powered*
die Windenergie	*wind energy*
die Windkraftanlage (n)	
	wind power station
das Windrad (·· er)	*wind turbine*

NATUR

das Aussterben	*extinction*
bedroht/gefährdet	*endangered*

beschädigen	*to damage*
das Fischsterben	*death of fish*
die Kontaminierung	*contamination*
die Luftverschmutzung	*air pollution*
der Naturschutz	*nature protection*
der Ölteppich (e)	*oil slick*
der Regenwald (·· er)	*rainforest*
retten	*to save*
schädigen	*to damage*
der Schutz	*protection*
schützen	*to protect*
vergiften	*to poison*
vergiftet	*poisoned*
das Waldsterben	*dying of forests*
das Walfangverbot (e)	
	ban on whale hunting
das Walschutzgebiet (e)	
	whale protected area
die Zerstörung (en)	*destruction*

die Regenwälder werden in rasender Geschwindigkeit abgeholzt	*the rain forests are being deforested at an alarming speed*
seltene Tierarten sterben aus	*rare species are dying out*
vom Aussterben bedroht	*at risk of extinction*
sich stark machen für	*to campaign for*
der Greenpeace-Aktivist	*Greenpeace activist*
das Handelsverbot für Walfleisch	*trade ban on whale meat*
gegen den Walfang protestieren	*to protest against whale hunting*
die Internationale Walfangkommission	*international whale hunting commission*
die Meere vor Überfischung schützen	*to protect the sea from over-fishing*

KLIMA

die Dürre	*drought*
das Erdbeben (-)	*earthquake*
das Hochwasser	*flooding*
das Klima (s)	*climate*
die Klimakatastrophe (n)	
	climate disaster
die Lawine (n)	*avalanche*
der Monsun (e)	*monsoon*
die Schlammlawine (n)	*mud slide*
der Taifun	*typhoon*
die Überschwemmung (en)	*flood*
das Unwetter (-)	*storm*
der Waldbrand (¨ e)	*forest fire*
der Wirbelsturm (¨ e)	*hurricane*

MÜLLBESEITIGUNG

die Abfallentsorgung (en)	
	waste disposal
Abfall vermeiden	*to avoid waste*
die Abfallvermeidung	*waste reduction*
das Altpapier	*waste paper*
der Bioabfall (¨ e)	*biological waste*
die Deponie (n)	*dump*
der Deponieraum (¨ e)	*disposal site*
die Entsorgung (en)	*waste management*
der Gartenabfall (¨ e)	*garden waste*
der Glascontainer (-)	*bottle bank*
der Komposthaufen (-)	*compost heap*
kompostieren	*to compost*
der Küchenabfall (¨ e)	*kitchen waste*

die Auswirkungen zu spüren bekommen	*to feel the effects*
die Aufheizung der Erdatmosphäre	*global warming*
die klimatische Veränderung (en)	*climate change*
der Meeresspiegel steigt	*sea levels are rising*
der sintflutartige Regen	*torrential rain*
kompostierfähiger Abfall	*compostable waste*
den Müll sortieren	*to sort your rubbish*
1993 wurde das Duale System eingeführt	*the Dual System was introduced in 1993*
Wertstoffe gehören in die grüne Tonne	*recyclable materials go in the green dustbin*
Bioabfall gehört in die braune Tonne	*bio-waste goes in the brown dustbin*
Restmüll gehört in die graue Tonne	*non-recyclable products go in the grey dustbin*
möglichst wenig Müll verursachen	*to create as little rubbish as possible*
durch den Verzicht auf Verpackungen	*by doing without packaging*
die Verpackungen tragen den grünen Punkt	*packaging displays the green sign*

die Landgewinnung	*land fill*
die Mehrwegverpackung (en)	*reusable packaging*
die Müllabfuhr	*rubbish collection*
die Müllkippe	*rubbish dump*
die Mülltonne (n)	*dustbin*
die Pfandflasche (n)	*returnable bottle*
das Recycling	*recycling*
das Recyclingpapier	*recycled paper*
der Sondermüll	*hazardous waste*
die Verpackung (en)	*packaging*
die Wiederverwertung	*reuse*

VERKEHR

die Autoabgase (pl)	*car exhaust fumes*
die Autobahnbenutzungsgebühr	*motorway toll*

die Busspur (en)	*bus lane*
das Carsharing System	*car-sharing scheme*
die Fahrgemeinschaft (en)	*carpool*
der Fahrradweg (e)	*cycle lane*
der Katalysator (en)	*catalytic converter*
der/die Pendler/in (-/nen)	*commuter*
der Stau (e)	*tailback*
die Stoßzeit (en)	*rush hour*
das Verkehrsaufkommen	*volume of traffic*
die Verkehrsinfrastruktur	*transport infrastructure*
der Verkehrsstau	*traffic congestion*
die Verkehrsvermeidung	*traffic avoidance*

autofreie Städte	*car-free cities*
der Zusammenhang zwischen Autoverkehr und Klimawandel	*the connection between car traffic and climate change*
überflüssigen Verkehr nicht entstehen lassen	*not to allow excess traffic to build up*
umweltfreundliche Verkehrsmittel	*environmentally-friendly modes of transport*
das bleifreie Benzin	*lead-free petrol*
die öffentlichen Verkehrsmittel (pl)	*public transport*
das Park und Ride System	*park and ride scheme*
die Maßnahmen zur Verkehrsberuhigung	*traffic-calming measures*
die Menschen auffordern, öffentliche Verkehrsmittel zu benutzen	*to encourage people to use public transport*

IN DER STADT

bebaut	*built-up*
die Fußgängerzone (n)	*pedestrian area*
der Geräuschpegel (-)	*noise level*
das Graffiti (-)	*graffiti*
der Grüngürtel (-)	*green belt*
heruntergekommen	*run-down*
die Innenstadt (⸚ e)	*inner city*
die Lärmminderung (en)	*noise reduction*
der Smog	*smog*
städtisch	*civic*
überbesiedelt	*overpopulated*
die Vorstadt (⸚ e)	*suburb*
die Wohnsiedlung (en)	*housing estate*
der Wolkenkratzer (-)	*sky-scraper*

AUF DEM LAND

abgeschieden	*isolated*
das Ackerland	*arable land*
die Agrokultur	*factory farming*
der Bauernhof (⸚ e)	*farm*
die Ernte (n)	*harvest*
ertragreich	*fertile*
erzeugen	*to produce*
die Landwirtschaft	*agriculture*
öde	*barren*
der Rinderwahnsinn	*BSE*
die Subvention (en)	*subsidy*
der Tierschützer	*animal rights activist*

innovative Stadtplanung	*imaginative town-planning*
städtische Gegenden neu beleben	*to regenerate urban areas*
Waldflächen in Brand setzen, um Ackerland zu erhalten	*setting forests alight to create arable land*
gegen Tierquälerei sein	*to be against cruelty to animals*
die nachhaltige Landwirtschaft	*sustainable farming*
die organische Landwirtschaft	*organic farming*
die Intensivlandwirtschaft	*intensive farming methods*
Landwirtschaft betreiben	*to farm*
die ländliche Siedlung	*rural community*

VOKABELTIPP

Wörterbuch: Englisch/Deutsch

Wenn Sie ein bestimmtes deutsches Wort suchen, schlagen Sie es im Wörterbuch nach. Achten Sie aber darauf, dass Sie das passende Wort wählen.

Sehen Sie diesen Auszug an und beantworten Sie die unten stehenden Fragen.

Lautschrift

Phrasen

Bedeutungen

Worttyp,
z.B. Substantiv,
Verb, usw.

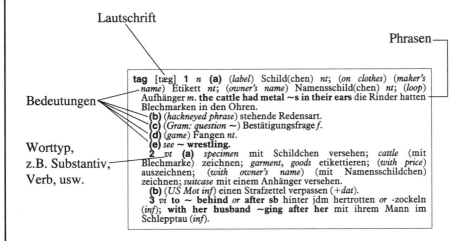

tag [tæg] **1** *n* **(a)** (*label*) Schild(chen) *nt*; (*on clothes*) (*maker's name*) Etikett *nt*; (*owner's name*) Namensschild(chen) *nt*; (*loop*) Aufhänger *m*. **the cattle had metal ~s in their ears** die Rinder hatten Blechmarken in den Ohren.
(b) (*hackneyed phrase*) stehende Redensart.
(c) (*Gram: question ~*) Bestätigungsfrage *f*.
(d) (*game*) Fangen *nt*.
(e) *see* ~ **wrestling.**
2 *vt* **(a)** *specimen* mit Schildchen versehen; *cattle* (mit Blechmarke) zeichnen; *garment, goods* etikettieren; (*with price*) auszeichnen; (*with owner's name*) (mit Namensschildchen) zeichnen; *suitcase* mit einem Anhänger versehen.
(b) (*US Mot inf*) einen Strafzettel verpassen (+*dat*).
3 *vi* **to ~ behind** *or* **after sb** hinter jdm hertrotten *or* -zockeln (*inf*); **with her husband ~ging after her** mit ihrem Mann im Schlepptau (*inf*).

a) Wie viele Bedeutungen hat *a tag* auf Deutsch?

b) Wie sagt man *he tags behind his father* auf Deutsch?

c) Wie heißt *a tag question* auf Deutsch?

d) Wie sagt man *to put a tag on a suitcase* auf Deutsch?

e) Was ist der Unterschied zwischen *Etikett* und *etikettieren*?

f) Was ist richtig: *der/die/das Fangen*?

Tipp! Wenn Sie ein neues deutsches Wort nachschlagen, überprüfen Sie es, indem Sie es auch im deutsch-englischen Wörterbuch nachschlagen.

WELTBLICKE

FRIEDEN

die Abrüstung	*disarmament*
die Abschreckung (en)	*deterrent*
die Feuerpause (n)	*ceasefire*
das Friedensabkommen (-)	*peace treaty*
die Friedensbewegung (en)	*peace movement*
die Friedenszeit (en)	*peace time*
die Kriegsverhinderung	*prevention of war*
das Ölembargo (s)	*oil embargo*
der Pazifismus	*pacifism*
der/die Pazifist/in (-/nen)	*pacifist*
die Rettungsaktion (en)	*rescue action*
die Verhandlungen (pl)	*negotiations*
der Wehrdienstverweigerer (-)	*conscientious objector*
der Weltfrieden	*world peace*
der Zivildienst	*community service (for conscientious objectors)*

KRIEG

der Angreifer (-)	*aggressor*
die Armee (n)	*army*
die Atombombe (n)	*atom bomb*
das Aufmarschgebiet (e)	*deployment area*
die Ausgangssperre (n)	*curfew*
besetzt	*occupied*
das Blutbad (⸚ er)	*blood bath*
die Bodentruppen (pl)	*ground forces*
der Bombenanschlag (⸚ e)	*bomb attack*
die Bundeswehr	*German army*
der Bürgerkrieg (e)	*civil war*
erobern	*to conquer*
erschrecken	*to terrify*
eskalieren	*to escalate*
evakuieren	*to evacuate*
die Exekution (en)	*execution*
die Feindseligkeit (en)	*hostility*
foltern	*to torture*
die Gasmaske (n)	*gas mask*

einem Land Sanktionen auferlegen	*to impose sanctions against a country*
die Landminen beseitigen	*to clear landmines*
die humanitäre Hilfe	*humanitarian aid*
Flüchtlingshilfe der Vereinten Nationen	*United Nations refugee aid*
diplomatische Beziehungen	*diplomatic relations*

der Gebietsverlust (e)	loss of territory	der Militärputsch (e)	military putsch
gefangennehmen	to take prisoner	die Mittelstreckenwaffe (n)	
der Gegenschlag (∸ e)	reprisal		medium range weapon
der Glaubenskrieg (e)	religious war	die Munition	ammunition
das Granatfeuer	shelling	der Nord-Süd-Konflikt (e)	
die Greueltat (en)	atrocity		north-south conflict
der Konflikt (e)	conflict	der Notstand (∸ e)	state of emergency
konventionell	conventional	die Rakete (n)	rocket
der Konvoi (s)	convoy	der Rüstungswettlauf	arms race
kriegführend	warring	schwer verletzt	seriously injured
das Kriegsopfer (-)	war victim	der/die Soldat/in (en/nen)	soldier
die Kurzstreckenwaffe (n)		der Sprengstoff (e)	explosive
	short range weapon	die Supermacht (∸ e)	superpower
die Leiche (n)	corpse	strategisch	strategic
der Luftangriff (e)	air raid	die Streitkräfte (pl)	forces
das Massaker (-)	massacre	die Tötung (en)	killing
die Massenvernichtung		übergeben	to surrender
	mass destruction	der/die Überlebende (n)	survivor
die Militärmacht (∸ e)	military power	die Unterwerfung	subjugation

das menschliche Schutzschild	human shield
bei Angriffen getötet werden	to be killed in attacks
ein langandauernder Konflikt	a lengthy conflict
schwere Kämpfe (pl)	heavy fighting
vor Erschöpfung sterben	to die of exhaustion
ethnische Säuberung	ethnic cleansing
lebenslange Schäden erleiden	to suffer lifelong injury
es brachte 300 Menschen den Tod	it killed 300 people
er fiel der Bombe zum Opfer	he was a victim of the bomb
militärische Intervention	military intervention
ins Kreuzfeuer geraten	to get caught in the crossfire
die Stadt steht unter Beschuss	the town is under fire

die Vernichtung	*extermination*
die Verdunkelung (en)	*blackout*
die Verteidigung	*defence*
der Waffenhandel	*arms trade*
der Waffenstillstand	*armistice*
der Wehrdienst	*military service*
zerstören	*to destroy*

RELIGION

anbeten	*to worship*
die Andacht (en)	*worship, prayer*
anglikanisch	*Anglican*
der/die Atheist/in (en/nen)	*atheist*
die Beerdigung (en)	*funeral*
bekehren (zu)	*to convert (to)*
die Berufung (en)	*mission, calling*
die Bibel (-)	*bible*
der Buddha	*Buddha*

der Buddhismus	*Buddhism*
der/die Buddhist/in (en/nen)	*Buddhist*
das Christentum	*Christianity*
der/die Christ/in (en/nen)	*Christian*
das Dogma (-men)	*dogma*
die Dreifaltigkeit	*trinity*
der Erlöser	*Saviour*
evangelisch	*Protestant*
der Friedhof (⸚ e)	*cemetery*
fromm	*devout*
das Gebet (e)	*prayer*
geistig	*spiritual*
der Glaube (n)	*faith*
der Gott (⸚ er)	*God*
der Gottesdienst (e)	*church service*
der Guru (s)	*guru*
das Heil	*salvation*
heilig	*holy*

der religiöse Fanatiker	*religious fanatic*
eine religiöse Versammlung	*a religious gathering*
gegen meine Religion verstoßen	*to be against my religion*
etwas im Namen der Religion machen	*to do something in the name of religion*
als Katholik auf die Welt kommen	*to be born a Catholic*
an ein Leben nach dem Tod glauben	*to believe in life after death*
ein gläubiger Mensch	*a believer*
der Sinn des Lebens	*the meaning of life*
die Unfehlbarkeit des Papstes	*the infallibility of the Pope*
zum/zur X konvertieren	*to convert to X*
an Gott glauben	*to believe in God*
aus der Kirche austreten	*to leave the Church*

der Himmel (-)	*heaven*	der Protestantismus	*Protestantism*
der Hinduismus	*Hinduism*	religiös	*religious*
der Hindu (s)	*Hindu*	die Seele (n)	*soul*
die Hoffnung (en)	*hope*	das Seelenleben	*spiritual life*
die Hölle (n)	*hell*	der Segen (-)	*blessing*
der Islam	*Islam*	die Sekte (n)	*sect*
das Judentum	*Judaism*	der/die Sünder/in (-/nen)	*sinner*
der Jude (n)	*Jew (m)*	die Synagoge (n)	*synagogue*
die Jüdin (nen)	*Jew (f)*	die Taufe (n)	*baptism*
der Kirchengänger	*churchgoer*	der Tempel (-)	*temple*
die Kommunion	*communion*	der Teufel (-)	*devil*
der Koran	*Koran*	die Theologie	*theology*
katholisch	*Catholic*	die Überzeugung (en)	*conviction*
der Kult (e)	*cult*	die Weltreligion (en)	*world religion*
der Lama (s)	*lama*	die Wiedergeburt (en)	*reincarnation*
die Meditation (en)	*meditation*	die Zeremonie (n)	*ceremony*
der/die Missionar/in (e/nen)	*missionary*		
die Moschee (n)	*mosque*		

DRITTE WELT

der Moslem (s)	*Moslem*
orthodox	*orthodox*
der Prophet (en)	*prophet*

die Armut	*poverty*
die Ausbeutung (en)	*exploitation*
benötigen	*to need, require*

die armen Länder verschulden sich immer weiter	*poor countries are getting ever deeper into debt*
der Schuldenerlass für Dritte-Welt-Länder	*cancelling of Third World debt*
auf Kosten der Dritten Welt leben	*to live at the expense of the Third World*
Hilfe zur Selbsthilfe	*helping people help themselves*
verschmutztes Wasser	*contaminated water*
medizinische Hilfe	*medical help*
die ärmsten Länder der Welt unterstützen	*to support the poorest countries in the world*

die Bevölkerungsexplosion (en)

population explosion

das Bevölkerungswachstum

population growth

der Bodenertrag (⁼ e) *crop yield*

das Dritte-Welt-Land (⁼ er)

Third World country

das Elend *misery*

der/die Entwicklungshelfer/in (-/nen)

development worker

die Entwicklungshilfe (n)

development aid

die Ernährung *nourishment*

die Familienplanung *family planning*

die Geburtenkontrolle (n)

birth control

die Geburtenrate (n) *birth rate*

die Hilfslieferung (en) *delivery of aid*

die Hilfsorganisation (en)

relief organisation

das Hilfsprogramm (e) *aid programme*

die Hungersnot (⁼ e) *famine*

die Industrialisierung (en)

industrialisation

die Krankheit (en) *disease*

das Krisengebiet (e) *crisis area*

die Malaria *malaria*

mangeln *to lack*

die Not (⁼ e) *need(iness), want*

die Naturkatastrophe (n)

natural disaster

das Nothilfeprogramm (e)

relief programme

das Notlager *emergency camp*

die Regenzeit (en) *rainy season*

die Schulden (pl) *debts*

der Slum (s) *slum*

die Spende (n) *donation*

die Überbevölkerung *overpopulation*

die Ungerechtigkeit (en) *injustice*

die Unterdrückung (en) *oppression*

unterentwickelt *underdeveloped*

die Unterernährung *malnourishment*

verdursten *to die of thirst*

verhungern *to starve*

die moralisch betonte Außenpolitik *ethical foreign policy*

zu den Bedürftigen kommen *to reach the needy*

die Weltbevölkerung wächst jeden Tag *the world population increases daily*

ein abgemagertes Kind *an emaciated child*

unter der Armutsgrenze leben *to live below the poverty line*

eine hohe Zahl von Analphabeten *a large number of illiterate people*

katastrophale Zustände *catastrophic circumstances*

niedrige Lebenserwartungen *low life expectancy*

EU

die Barriere (n)	*barrier*
die Bürokratie	*bureaucracy*
die Demokratie	*democracy*
Einheit in Vielfalt	*unity in diversity*
die einzige Währung	*single currency*
der EU-Erlass	*EU directive*
den Euro akzeptieren	*to accept the Euro*
der/die Europäer/in (-/nen)	*European (person)*
Europäische Kommission	*European Commission*
Europäischer Binnenmarkt	*Common Market*
Europäischer Gerichtshof	*European Court of Justice*
Europäischer Rat	*European Council*

Europäisches Parlament	*European Parliament*
Europäische Union	*European Union*
Europäische Zentralbank	*European Central Bank*
der/die Euroskeptiker/in (-/nen)	*Eurosceptic*
die Eurozone	*the Eurozone*
die Freizügigkeit	*freedom of movement*
der Grenzabbau	*removal of borders*
die Kompensation (en)	*compensation*
der Kontinent (e)	*continent*
der Ministerrat	*Council of Ministers*
der Mitgliedsstaat (en)	*member state*
der Pluralismus	*pluralism*
die Subvention (en)	*subsidy*
der Überschuss (¨ e)	*surplus*
die Zusammenarbeit	*collaboration*

Mitglied der Europäischen Union	*member of the European Union*
die Wirtschafts- und Währungsunion	*economic and currency union*
die europäische Währungsunion	*European monetary union*
ein Europa der zwei Geschwindigkeiten	*two-speed Europe*
Wohnsitz, Ausbildungsort und Arbeitsplatz frei wählen	*to choose where to live, study and work*
das Gesicht Europas prägen	*to shape the face of Europe*
steuerliche Schranken abbauen	*to remove tax barriers*
Gemeinsame Agrarpolitik (GAP)	*Common Agricultural Policy (CAP)*
der Europarat der Menschenrechte	*European Court of Human Rights*

Zusammengesetzte Wörter (2)

Ein zusammengesetztes Wort besteht aus zwei oder mehreren Wörtern.

Das Geschlecht des Wortes wird vom letzten Teil bestimmt.

Zum Beispiel *Jugendzentrum* besteht aus zwei Wörtern:

die Jugend (f)/das Zentrum (n)

Da *Zentrum* neutrum ist, ist *Jugendzentrum* auch neutrum.

a) Sind die Wörter unten maskulinum, femininum oder neutrum?

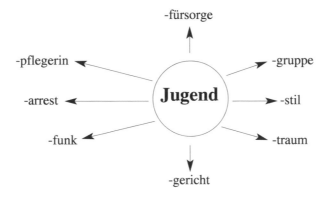

b) Was bedeuten die Wörter auf Englisch?

Wie viele zusammengesetzte Wörter können Sie für Tier-, Mutter-
und Kopf- finden? Machen Sie eine Liste davon!

WIRTSCHAFT

AUF DER BANK

das Bankwesen	*banking*
das Bargeld	*cash*
bargeldlos	*cashless*
die Bausparkasse (n)	*building society*
brutto	*gross*
das Darlehen (-)	*loan*
einlösen	*to cash (a cheque)*
die Filiale (n)	*branch*
die Forderung (en)	*demand*
die Gebühr (en)	*fee, charge*
die Geheimzahl (en)	*PIN number*
der Geldautomat (en)	*cash dispenser*
das Girokonto (-ten)	*current account*
gutschreiben	*to credit*
die Hypothek (en)	*mortgage*
das Internetbanking	*internet banking*
die Kaution (en)	*deposit*

der Kontoauszug (¨ e)	*bank statement*
die Kontobewegung (en)	*bank transaction*
der Kredit (e)	*credit, loan*
die Kreditgrenze (n)	*credit limit*
der Kredithai	*loan shark*
die Kreditkarte (n)	*credit card*
netto	*net*
pleite	*bankrupt*
die Scheckkarte (n)	*cheque card*
das Sparkonto (-ten)	*savings account*
überweisen	*to transfer*
überziehen	*to overdraw*
zahlungsfähig	*solvent*
zahlungsunfähig	*insolvent*
die Zinsen (pl)	*interest*
das Zinsenkonto (-ten)	*interest account*

Xs Konto mit einer Summe belasten	*to debit X's account with a sum*
per Dauerauftrag bezahlen	*to pay by standing order*
das lasse ich mir vom Konto abbuchen	*I will have that debited from my account*
bei Barzahlung 2% Skonto	*2% cash discount*
in bar bezahlen	*to pay by cash*
eine Rechnung begleichen	*to settle an invoice*
nach Abzug von Steuern	*after tax*
in den roten Zahlen sein (inf)	*to be in the red*

WIRTSCHAFT

die Analyse (n)	*analysis*
der Aufschwung (⸚ e)	*upturn*
der Auftrieb (e)	*upward trend*
die Ausgabe (n)	*expenditure*
der Außenhandel	*foreign trade*
die Aussicht (en)	*prospect*
das Budget (s)	*budget*
das Defizit (e)	*deficit*
effektiv	*in real terms*
die Einkommenssteuer	*income tax*
die Einsparung (en)	*cost-cutting*
der Einzelhandelspreisindex	*retail price index*
die Erneuerung	*regeneration*
der Ertrag (⸚ e)	*yield*
der Exportmarkt (⸚ e)	*export market*

die Flaute (n)	*depression*
die Handelsbilanz (en)	*balance of trade*
die Hochkonjunktur (en)	*boom*
die Inflationsrate (n)	*rate of inflation*
die Konjunktur (en)	*economic situation*
der Konkurrent (en)	*competitor*
die Konkurrenz (en)	*competition*
konkurrenzfähig	*competitive*
die Körperschaftssteuer	*corporation tax*
die Kosten (pl)	*costs*
der Lebenshaltungskostenindex	*cost-of-living index*
der Leitzins (en)	*base rate*
die Mehrwertsteuer (MwSt)	*Value Added Tax (VAT)*

freie Marktwirtschaft	*free market economy*
soziale Marktwirtschaft	*social market economy*
Steuererhöhungen durchsetzen	*to raise taxes*
die Inflationsrate ist auf 4,1% gefallen	*the inflation rate has fallen to 4.1%*
das Staatsdefizit soll sinken	*the national deficit should be reduced*
die Wirtschaft ankurbeln	*to boost the economy*
von 34 auf 36% erhöhen	*to raise from 34 to 36%*
konjunkturell bedingt	*due to economic factors*
die boomende und absteigende Wirtschaft	*boom and bust economy*
eine nachhaltige Verbesserung	*a sustained recovery*

die Nationalschuld	*national debt*	die Wirtschaftslage	*economic climate*
ökonomisch	*economical*	das Wirtschaftswunder (-)	
die Planwirtschaft	*planned economy*		*economic miracle*
der Preisanstieg (e)	*price increase*	die Wirtschaftskrise (n)	
der Preisnachlass (⁔ e)	*price reduction*		*economic crisis*
die Rezession (en)	*recession*	die Zahlungsbilanz (en)	
rückläufig	*declining*		*balance of payments*
die Schulden (pl)	*debts*		

die Sozialabgaben (pl)

AN DER BÖRSE

	welfare contributions	die Aktie (n)	*share*
die Steuer (n)	*tax*	die Aktienanteile (pl)	*stock options*
die Steuerbelastung (en)	*tax burden*	der Aktienhöchststand	*all-time high*
die Vermögensverteilung		der Aktientiefstand	*all-time low*
	distribution of wealth	der/die Aktionär/in (e/nen)	*shareholder*
der/die Volkswirt/in (e/-nen)		die Anlage (n)	*investment*
	economist	anlegen	*to invest*
das Wachstum	*growth*	die Anleihe (n)	*bond*
die Wirtschaft	*economy*	der Anteil (e)	*holding*

das Portfolio diversifizieren	*to diversify your portfolio*
die Marktunsicherheit	*uncertainty in the marketplace*
der Deutsche Aktienindex (Dax)	*German stock market index (Dax)*
an der Börse Geld verlieren/verdienen	*to lose/make money on the stock exchange*
der Abwärtstrend ist nicht zu stoppen	*the downward trend cannot be halted*
einen neuen Höchstwert erreichen	*to reach a new high*
mit Anleihen verdient man brutto 7%	*you earn 7% gross with bonds*
in Aktien investieren	*to invest in shares*
einen drastischen Rückgang zu verzeichnen haben	*to report a drastic drop*
der steigende Kurs	*stock price increase*

die Börse (n)	*stock market*
die Dividende (n)	*dividend*
die Finanzierung (en)	*finance*
der Fonds (-)	*fund*
der Gewinn (e)	*profit*
das Insidergeschäft (e)	
	insider dealing
der Internethandel	*internet trading*
investieren	*to invest*
die Investition (en)	*investment*
der Investor (en)	*investor*
das Kapital	*capital*
der Kurs (e)	*rate, price*
der Kurseinbruch (¨ e)	
	stock market crash
die Kursverluste (pl)	*losses*
der/die Makler/in (-/nen)	*broker*
online investieren	*to invest online*
das Portfolio	*portfolio*

die Privatisierung (en)	*privatisation*
spekulieren	*to speculate*
die Technologieaktie (n)	
	technology stock
die Termingeschäfte (pl)	*futures*
die Transaktionen (pl)	*dealing*
volatil	*volatile*

HANDEL

Abstriche machen	*to make cutbacks*
die Branche (n)	*sector*
der Betrieb (e)	*business, firm*
die Dienstleistung (en)	*service*
die Dienstleistungsbranche (n)	
	service industry
der Einzelhandel	*retail trade*
erzeugen	*to produce*
das Erzeugnis (se)	*product*

die AG (Aktiengesellschaft)	*Plc (Public Limited Company)*
Angebot und Nachfrage	*supply and demand*
mit Briten treiben wir viel Handel	*we do a lot of business with the British*
die allgemeinen Geschäftsbedingungen	*terms of trade*
Gesellschaft mit beschränkter Haftung (GmbH)	*private limited company (Ltd)*
ein Unternehmen mit einem Jahresumsatz von mehr als . . .	*a firm with an annual turnover of more than . . .*
sie importierten Waren im Wert von . . .	*they imported goods to a value of . . .*
das Geschäft wirft jetzt Gewinn ab	*the business is now running at a profit*
in Konkurs gehen	*to go bankrupt*

der Export (e)	*export*
exportieren	*to export*
die Fertigung (en)	*production*
der Fertigungsausstoß	
	manufacturing output
die Gewerkschaft (en)	*trade union*
die Globalisierung	*globalisation*
der Großhandel	*wholesale trade*
die Handelskammer (n)	
	chamber of commerce
herstellen	*to manufacture*
die Herstellung (en)	*manufacturing*
die High-Tech-Industrie	
	high-tech industry
der Import (e)	*import*
die Industrie (n)	*industry*
das Marketing	*marketing*
der Marktanteil (e)	*market share*
der Marktführer (-)	*market leader*
der Marktplatz (⸚ e)	*marketplace*

die Massenproduktion	
	mass production
die Messe (n)	*trade fair*
das Monopol (e)	*monopoly*
das Sortiment (e)	*product range*
die Sparte (n)	*line of business*
die Telekommunikationsmarkt	
	telecommunications market
die Tochtergesellschaft (en)	
	subsidiary
die Übernahme (n)	*takeover*
das Unternehmen (-)	*company*
der/die Unternehmer/in (-/nen)	
	entrepreneur
der Unternehmergeist	
	entrepreneurial spirit
unternehmerisch	*entrepreneurial*
vermarkten	*to market*
die Ware (n)	*goods*
das Werk (e)	*works, factory*

VOKABELTIPP

Lernstrategien

Wenn Sie Ihren Wortschatz erweitern wollen, helfen Ihnen Lernstrategien.
Wahrscheinlich haben Sie sich dafür schon einige Strategien ausgedacht. Hier
sind noch mehr Ideen, die Ihnen weiterhelfen.

a) Lernen Sie jeden Tag fünf neue Wörter. Am Ende der Woche versuchen Sie,
sie alle aufzuschreiben. Die Wörter, die Sie inzwischen vergessen haben,
können Sie dann wieder in der nächsten Woche lernen.

b) Nehmen Sie die deutschen Wörter zu einem bestimmten Thema auf Kassette
auf. Lassen Sie nach jedem Wort eine Pause. Dann fügen Sie die englische
Bedeutung ein. Wenn Sie unterwegs sind, können Sie die Kassette im Walkman
abhören. Sagen Sie das englische Wort, bevor Sie es nach der Pause hören. Sie
können das dann natürlich auch umgekehrt machen: Englisch – Deutsch!

c) Schreiben Sie die Vokabeln zu bestimmten Themen auf kleine Karten:
Schreiben Sie das deutsche Wort auf eine Seite der Karte und das englische
Wort auf die andere. Legen Sie die Karten auf den Tisch und geben Sie die
richtige Übersetzung an. Wiederholen Sie das Spiel von Zeit zu Zeit.

PHRASEN

ZEITAUSDRÜCKE

ab und zu	*now and again*
andauernd	*constantly*
die Ära (Ären)	*era*
danach	*after that*
davor	*before that*
die Epoche (n)	*epoch*
die Festzeit (en)	*festive season*
gestern	*yesterday*
häufig	*often*
heute	*today*
im Hochsommer	
	at the height of summer
das Jahrhundert (e)	*century*
die Jahrhundertwende (n)	
	turn of the century

das Jahrzehnt (e)	*decade*
das Jubiläum (-äen)	*anniversary*
der Kalendermonat (e)	
	calendar month
kaum	*rarely*
das Millennium	*millennium*
am Monatsende	
	at the end of the month
nach wie vor	*still*
pünktlich	*punctually*
das Schaltjahr (e)	*leap year*
der Sonnenaufgang (- e)	*sunrise*
der Sonnenuntergang (- e)	*sunset*
sporadisch	*sporadically*
bei Tagesanbruch	*at dawn*
tagtäglich	*day in day out*

die besten Jahre deines Lebens	*the best years of your life*
die Spuren der Zeit	*the ravages of time*
das Leben im 21. Jahrhundert	*life in the 21st century*
auf das Jahr zurückschauen	*to look back over the year*
ein erfolgreiches neues Jahr	*a successful new year*
einen guten Rutsch ins Neue Jahr	*Happy New Year*
im Großen und Ganzen war das Jahr . . .	*on the whole the year has been . . .*
in den kommenden Jahren	*in the coming years*
von der Zeit an	*from that time on*
vor Jahren lebte ich in London	*years ago I lived in London*
das ist Jahre her	*that is years ago*

übermorgen	*the day after tomorrow*
vorgestern	*the day before yesterday*
das Wochenende (n)	*weekend*
der Wochentag (e)	*weekday*
zur Zeit	*at the moment*

FÜLLWÖRTER

allerdings	*mind you*
alles in allem	*all in all*
als je zuvor	*than ever before*
am Anfang/Ende	*at the beginning/end*
an deiner Stelle	*in your position*
andererseits	*on the other hand*
angeblich	*supposedly*
apropos	*talking of*
auf alle Fälle	*in any case*
auf keinen Fall	*on no account*
außerdem	*furthermore*
beispielsweise	*for instance*

einerseits	*on the one hand*
erst wenn	*only when*
es sei denn	*unless*
gewiss	*certain*
hauptsächlich	*mainly*
kein Kommentar	*no comment*
im allgemeinen	*in general*
im Alltag	*in day to day life*
im Durchschnitt	*on average*
im Ernst	*seriously*
im Gegensatz zu	*as opposed to*
im Gegenteil	*on the contrary*
im Grunde	*basically*
im Nachhinein	*in retrospect*
im Prinzip	*in principle*
im Vergleich zu	*compared with*
im Widerspruch zu	*contrary to*
in der Hoffnung, dass	*in the hope that*
in der Tat	*in fact*

vor langer Zeit lernte ich Deutsch	*long ago I learned German*
das ist lange her	*that is long ago*
vor einer Weile habe ich sie gesehen	*a while ago I saw her*
das ist eine Weile her	*that is a while ago*
alles zu seiner Zeit	*all in good time*
die Zeit vergeht	*time ticks by*
so gut wie kaum	*hardly ever*
Punkt elf	*at eleven o'clock on the dot*
am frühen/späten Abend	*in the early/late evening*
in vierzehn Tagen	*in a fortnight*
alle Jubeljahre	*once in a blue moon*

in Sicht	*in sight*	unbestritten	*indisputable*
insofern als	*in so far as*	unheimlich	*incredibly*
in Wirklichkeit	*in reality*	vergeblich	*in vain*
jedenfalls	*in any case*	vermutlich	*presumably*
keineswegs	*on no account*	verständlicherweise	*understandably*
kurz gesagt	*in short*	von da an	*from then on*
mit der Aussicht auf	*with the view to*	vor allem	*above all*
möglicherweise	*possibly*	voraussichtlich	*expected, probably*
nachträglich	*subsequently*	vorwiegend	*predominantly*
offenbar	*apparently*	wesentlich	*considerably*
ohnehin	*anyway*	wie immer	*as ever*
selbstverständlich	*obviously*	zu Anfang	*to begin with*
sogenannt	*so-called*	zum Glück	*luckily*
stattdessen	*instead of that*	zum Großteil	*in the main*
tatsächlich	*actually*	zumindest	*at least*
übrigens	*by the way*	zusätzlich	*additionally*
umgekehrt	*vice versa*	zweifellos	*doubtless*

in einer Krise stecken	*to be in a crisis*
es kommt darauf an	*it depends*
es ist mir egal	*I don't care*
es ist mir gleich	*it's all the same to me*
etwas objektiv/subjektiv betrachten	*to view something objectively/subjectively*
etwas im Blick haben	*to have something in mind*
zum Ziel kommen	*to achieve the objective*
eine Reihe von Gründen	*a lot of reasons*
in einer Untersuchung heißt es . . .	*according to an investigation . . .*
laut eines Berichts	*according to a report*
Schlussfolgerungen ziehen	*to draw conclusions*
erstens/zweitens/drittens	*firstly/secondly/thirdly*
es entspricht nicht den Tatsachen	*it's not in accordance with the facts*

MEINUNGEN

ich akzeptiere, dass . . .	*I accept that . . .*
ich befürchte, dass . . .	*I fear that . . .*
ich behaupte, dass . . .	*I claim that . . .*
ich bezweifle, dass . . .	*I doubt that . . .*
ich bin der Meinung, dass . . .	*I think that . . .*
ich bin für/gegen . . .	*I'm for/against . . .*
ich bin entsetzt, dass . . .	*I'm horrified that . . .*
ich bin skeptisch gegenüber . . .	*I'm sceptical about . . .*
ich bin stolz, dass . . .	*I'm proud that . . .*
ich bin überzeugt, dass. . .	*I'm convinced that . . .*
ich finde, dass . . .	*I find that . . .*
ich gebe zu, dass . . .	*I admit that . . .*
ich glaube, dass . . .	*I believe that . . .*
ich habe den Eindruck, dass . . .	*I have the impression that . . .*
ich habe keinerlei Interesse an . . .	*I'm not remotely interested in . . .*
ich habe keinen Zweifel, dass . . .	*I don't have any doubt that . . .*
ich halte es für möglich, dass . . .	*I think it's possible that . . .*
ich hoffe, dass . . .	*I hope that . . .*
ich lege Wert darauf, dass . . .	*I think it's important that . . .*
ich meine, dass . . .	*I think that . . .*
ich möchte feststellen, ob . . .	*I would like to ascertain whether . . .*
ich nehme an, dass . . .	*I assume that . . .*
ich nehme es ernst, dass . . .	*I take it seriously that . . .*
ich schlage vor, dass . . .	*I suggest that . . .*
ich schließe es nicht aus, dass . . .	*I don't rule out the fact that . . .*
ich sehe eine Möglichkeit . . .	*I see a possibility . . .*
ich stimme zu, dass . . .	*I agree that . . .*
ich vermute, dass . . .	*I suspect that . . .*
ich wette, dass . . .	*I bet that . . .*
wir sind uns einig, dass . . .	*we're agreed that . . .*
meiner Meinung nach . . .	*in my opinion . . .*
wir gehen davon aus, dass . . .	*we assume that . . .*

ARGUMENTATIONEN

die Folge ist, dass . . .	*the consequence is that . . .*
das beweist, dass . . .	*that proves that . . .*
das führt dazu, dass . . .	*that leads to . . .*
das Gleiche gilt für . . .	*the same goes for . . .*
das ist der Grund, warum . . .	*that's the reason why . . .*
es betrifft . . .	*it concerns . . .*
es bleibt zu beachten, was . . .	*it remains to be seen what . . .*
es freut mich, dass . . .	*I am pleased that . . .*
es geht (nicht) um . . .	*it's (not) about . . .*
es handelt sich um . . .	*it's about . . .*
es hat keinen Sinn, dass . . .	*there's no point in . . .*
es ist bedauerlich, dass . . .	*it's regrettable that . . .*
es ist bekannt, dass . . .	*it's known that . . .*
es ist fraglich, ob . . .	*it's questionable whether . . .*
es ist klar, dass . . .	*it's clear that . . .*
es ist nicht wahr, dass . . .	*it's not true that . . .*
es ist nicht zu glauben, dass . . .	*it's not to be believed that . . .*
es ist die Rede von . . .	*there's talk of . . .*
es ist schwer vorstellbar, dass . . .	*it's hard to imagine that . . .*
es ist undenkbar, dass . . .	*it's inconceivable that . . .*
es ist völlig ausgeschlossen, dass . . .	*it's completely out of the question that . .*
es kann sein, dass . . .	*it can be that . . .*
es kommt darauf an, was. . .	*it depends on what . . .*
es lässt sich daraus schließen, dass . . .	*it leads to the conclusion that . . .*
es leuchtet ein, dass . . .	*it stands to reason that . . .*
es lenkt den Blick auf . . .	*it draws your attention to . . .*
es muss betont werden, dass . . .	*it must be stressed that . . .*
es steht fest, dass . . .	*one thing for sure, is that . . .*
es stellt sich heraus, dass . . .	*it turns out that . . .*
es stimmt nicht, dass . . .	*it's not true that . . .*
es wäre ratsam, . . .	*it would be advisable . . .*
es wird behauptet, dass . . .	*it's claimed that . . .*

JUGENDSZENE

Er ist ganz schön crazy.	*He's really way out.*
Er ist voll der Hunk.	*He's a real hunk.*
Hier geht echt die Post ab!	*The atmosphere here is great!*
Hier ist Tote Hose.	*There's nothing going on here.*
Ich bezahle diese Runde.	*This round's on me.*
Sie ist blau/besoffen/zu.	*She is drunk.*
Er ist hackezu.	*He is completely smashed.*
Ich fahre voll auf die Musik von X ab!	*I adore X's music!*
Der Typ hat mich angegraben.	*That bloke chatted me up.*
Er hat mich zugetextet.	*He talked my head off.*
Das war eine krasse/fette/geile Fete!	*That was a wicked/cool/mean party!*
Heute wollen wir die Sau rauslassen.	*We're going to let rip today.*
Ich gehe mit X.	*I'm going out with X.*
Ich bin verknallt in/echt scharf auf X.	*I'm madly in love with/I really fancy X.*
X ist ihr Schwarm.	*She's got a crush on X.*
Das Essen schmeckt voll korrekt!	*The meal is excellent!*
Ich komme nicht aus der Falle/Koje.	*I can't get out of bed.*
Der Lehrer ist echt ein Spießer.	*The teacher is a real bore.*
Sie labert uns ständig an.	*She's constantly getting at us.*
Ich habe null Bock, das zu tun.	*I don't feel like doing that.*
Das ist doch out.	*That's totally pointless.*
Ich hab's gecheckt!	*I've got it.*
Ich bin total gefrustet/echt genervt.	*I'm totally frustrated/at the end of my tether.*
Ich bin voll gestresst.	*I'm completely stressed out.*
Ich glaub', es hackt!	*You can't be serious!*
Logo!/Klaro!	*Of course!*
Du hast wohl 'n Rad ab!	*You've got a screw missing!*
Du tickst nicht richtig!/Du spinnst.	*You're off your rocker!/You're crazy.*
Alles in Ordnung?	*All right?*

Wenn man (allgemein) etwas toll findet, wählt man aus den folgenden Ausdrücken einen aus: *crazy, geil, gediegen, korrekt, stylisch, krass* (great/brilliant/brill/mega...). Und das meist mit dem Zusatz *echt* davor.

INTERNETADRESSEN

Starting points for websurfing
www.yahoo.de
www.netscape.com/de
www.compuserve.de

Dictionaries/vocabulary sites
www.compuserve.de/computingwelt
/internet/weblexikon/
http://sps.k12.mo.us/khs/german/
vocab/dtvocab.htm

German newspapers
www.faz.de
www.woche.de
www.welt.de
www.tz-online.de

German magazines
www.spiegel.de
www.focus.de
www.diezeit.de

German television stations
www.dwelle.de
www.ard.de
www.zdf.de

German political parties
Bündnis 90/Die Grünen:
www.gruene.de

Christlich Demokratische Union
Deutschlands (CDU): **www.cdu.de**
Freie Demokratische Partei
Deutschlands (F.D.P.):
www.liberale.de
Sozialdemokratische Partei
Deutschlands (SPD): **www.spd.de**

Greenpeace Germany:
www.greenpeace.de

German School web: **www.schule.de**

German government departments
Presse- und Informationsamt der
Bundesregierung:
www.government.de

Bundesamt für den Zivildienst:
www.zivildienst.de

Bundesamt für die Anerkennung
ausländischer Flüchtlinge:
www.bafl.de

Bundesamt für Naturschutz:
www.bfn.de

Umweltbundesamt:
www.umweltbundesamt.de

Bundesamt für die Sicherheit in der
Informationstechnik:
www.bsi.bund.de

Auswärtiges Amt:
www.auswaertiges-amt.de

Bundesministerium des Innern:
www.bmi.bund.de

Bundesministerium der Justiz:
www.bmj.bund.de

Bundesministerium der Finanzen:
www.bundesfinanzministerium.de

Bundesministerium für Familie,
Senioren, Frauen und Jugend:
www.bmfsfj.de

Bundesministerium für Wirtschaft und
Technologie: **www.bmwi.de**

Bundesministerium für Ernährung,
Landwirtschaft und Forsten:
www.bml.de

Bundesministerium für Arbeit und
Sozialordnung: **www.bma.bund.de**

Bundesministerium für Verkehr-, Bau-
und Wohnungswesen:
www.bmvbw.de

Bundesministerium der Verteidigung:
www.bundeswehr.de

Bundesministerium für Gesundheit:
www.bmgesundheit.de

Bundesministerium für wirtschaftliche
Zusammenarbeit und Entwicklung:
www.bmz.de

Bundesministerium für Bildung und
Forschung: **www.bmbf.de**

Bundesministerium für Umwelt,
Naturschutz und Reaktorsicherheit:
www.bmu.de

Austrian search engines
www.a-site.at
www.austronaut.at
www.softsurf.com/

Austrian tourist board:
http://austria-tourism.at
Vienna Online:
http://vienna-online.com/
Österreichische Rundfunk: **oe3.orf.at**

Some starting points for Switzerland
General site/search engine:
www.thebluewindow.ch
www.search.ch
Zürich Online: **www.zhol.ch**
Newspaper index:
www.portalino.ch/zeitungen/
index.asp

LÖSUNGEN

Seite 13
a) Aus (*out*) puff (*puff*) Gase (*gases*) = *exhaust fumes*; b) Arbeit (*work*) Geber (*giver*) = *employer*; c) Umwelt (*environment*) Verschmutzung (*pollution*) = environmental pollution; d) Taschen (*pocket*) Buch (*book*) = *paperback*; e) Hand (*hand*) Schuh (*shoe*) = *glove*; f) Fußgänger (*pedestrian*) unter (*under*) Führung (*guidance*) = *pedestrian subway*

Seite 24
zum Beispiel (*for example*), zu Händen (*for the attention of*), und so weiter (*etcetera*), Personenkraftwagen (*car*), vor allem (*above all*), das heißt (*that is*), und viele(s) andere (*and many more*), beziehungsweise (*or rather*), und ähnliches (*and similar*)

Seite 29
a) Karten; b) 5 – card, ticket, map, menu, playing card; c) die; d) wine list; e) He read my cards. f) She laid her cards on the table.

Seite 37
a) die Mitternacht (*midnight*); b) der Tagesanbruch (*daybreak*); c) die Geschäftsleute (*business people*); d) die Geburtstagskarte (*birthday card*)

Seite 57
a) knowledge; b) to get to know; c) expert; d) like an expert; e) code name; f) number plate, mark; g) code number

Seite 75
a) fünf; b) Er trottet hinter seinem Vater her. c) eine Bestätigungsfrage; d) Einen Koffer mit einem Anhänger versehen. e) Etikett ist ein Substantiv und etikettieren ist ein Verb. f) das

Seite 82
die Jugendfürsorge (*youth welfare*), die Jugendgruppe (*youth group*), der Jugendstil (*Art Nouveau*), der Jugendtraum (*youthful dream*), das Jugendgericht (*juvenile court*), der Jugendfunk (*radio for young people*), der Jugendarrest (*young offenders' detention*), die Jugendpflegerin (*female youth worker*)

NOTIZEN

NOTIZEN

NOTIZEN